SURVIVOR OF SILENCE

A POIGNANT JOURNEY, DISCOVERY AND RECOVERY FROM LIFE WITH DEAF PARENTS, A DEAF SISTER AND SEXUAL ABUSE

It took over half a century to untie the knots of silence…

I0973250

Dear Peg~

Hope you enjoy

reading this...

Sincerely

Ben

SURVIVOR OF SILENCE

A POIGNANT JOURNEY, DISCOVERY AND RECOVERY FROM LIFE WITH DEAF PARENTS, A DEAF SISTER AND SEXUAL ABUSE

BY

BENSON DAVID GARFINKLE-EVANS, Ph.D.

Bookstand Publishing

www.bookstandpublishing.com

Published by
Bookstand Publishing
Morgan Hill, CA 95037
3156_4

ISBN 978-1-58909-747-6

Printed in the United States of America

ACKNOWLEDGEMENTS:

This book has been sixty three years in the making and I am proud to share my truth and life's experiences with you in hopes that my experiences will make a difference in someone else's life. No one should ever have to live with guilt or shame. It is our God given right to live in our own authenticity.

Ketina "Mama" Brown- I would like to acknowledge the love, support and vision of my dear friend. Without her support this book would not have been written.

Brian Maxwell-Thank you, Brian, for assisting me in the editing of the book. You are a true friend.

Children of Deaf Adults-I acknowledge all the children of deaf adults (CODAs). There is a common thread that brings us together. Many of you have become very active in the deaf community and I applaud your efforts.

My heartfelt thoughts always remain with the deaf community. Although the challenges are considerably less than those in the time period of this writing, I realize they still exist. Fortunately, with amazing technology communication with the hearing community is much easier and more efficient. Today the deaf can achieve whatever profession they want.

DEDICATIONS:

My parents were brave, proud, and strong people. My father, Max, was an example of a person who accepted his deafness and was content and happy. My mother, Nettie, was uncomfortable with being deaf and this affected her self- esteem in a negative way. I regret her sadness. Her admiration and love for her children and grandchildren will always remain in our hearts. Mother and Dad, may you rest in peace.

To my children, Gayle and Bryan: Your devotion and love toward me is overwhelming. I behold your unique individuality. I love you.

To my grandsons Dylan and Jacob: May you grow to understand and appreciate your deaf heritage and your own individuality. You bring me such joy.

To my late and beloved former wife, Marsha Rener Garfinkle: Your understanding, compassion, and steadfast friendship will remain in my heart for eternity.

TABLE OF CONTENTS

INTRODUCTIONS

In a perfect world there is a wide range of new and exciting things open to exploration by a four year old. Playing games with friends, riding bikes, digging in the dirt, making mud pies, and just plain fun is what life at that age should be. But my life wasn't part of a 'perfect world.' I was a child born into 'silence' with deaf parents and a deaf sister.

In a perfect world parents are teachers, teaching children the ways of the world with its realities, both good and bad. Children need to feel protected by parents who help them develop a sense of security and self-confidence. I neither felt protected nor secure. There was challenge after challenge, and mine was a childhood lost. Parents and siblings are the most important part of a child's life. They set the tone for love, morality, responsibility, and values and I truly loved mine.

Four years old; what a joyful happy-go-lucky and impressionable age though it wasn't for me; I had to be mature beyond my age. Imagine at the age of four having to call doctors' offices to schedule medical appointments, to call neighbors and family for help, and to be available at anytime as the voice and ears through which your parents and sister communicate to the 'outside' world; the world of the hearing.

Mine was not a world where Blackberry phones, the internet, email, instant messaging, pagers, TDDs, and video conferencing existed.

These exceptional products and services of contemporary technology weren't around to assist the deaf in their need to communicate; the silent world I shared with my deaf family. My world was a dichotomy.

One half was me in the silent world of my parents and sister. The other was me in the world of the hearing. I straddled both worlds as a child with adult responsibilities.

Can you imagine living between two worlds and never feeling you belong to one or the other? I felt exactly that way. One world was silent and the deaf communicated via sign language with each other. They wrote notes and read the lips of the people in the hearing world. Hearing people would respond by shouting (as if *THAT* were going to work), writing notes, and developing their own admirable and oh-so-silly finger signs.

I learned at a very early age by my over-protective grandmother that my family *was* different and would always need me to be there for them. It is an understatement that I learned the concept of responsibility way too early. The impact is something that to this day has not totally left me. The positive effect of growing up in my family is that it became an integral part in shaping the unique individual I have become.

I wonder what my life would have been like had I not had been born into this very special family. And how would life have appeared if I were born into a 'normal' family? Would I have had more fun, less fear and taken life less seriously? Would my career have been different than what it was? Would I have been protected from sexual abuse? What would life turn out to be? One thing is for sure...I'll never know. It was not the life and purpose that God set forth for me.

I experienced many emotional conflicts and loss. The most devastating was the loss of my childhood. A 'normal' childhood would always be foreign to me. Depression, resentment, and sadness were not uncommon; even as a child.

Fortunately, as I grew older I realized my strength. I am a survivor who overcame the embarrassment, ridicule, and shame just because my family was different. Who I am today, for the most part, is a result of growing up in the world that I call the 'world of silence'.

There are a number of books written by CODAs (Children of Deaf Adults). I've read many of them and certainly relate to the individual plight of the authors. It appears to me that most of the children of deaf adults become adults who continue the affiliation and interaction with the deaf community by choosing careers related to helping the deaf. Many become interpreters, teachers, and counselors for the deaf. I admire all CODAs; especially those who remain active in the deaf community.

The effect and results of this special childhood, for me, is somewhat different. Truthfully, I anticipated the day that I would be free from the sometimes grandiose burden of being a hearing child. I felt alienated from the deaf community due to my parents deaths. The alienation, I will admit, was a welcome change. I needed to appropriately develop my self-identity which previously centered on being the son of deaf parents and the brother of a deaf sister. After my parents passing I wanted to live in my world, the world of the hearing, and find my own identity. Discovering my own identity apart from being a care giver was a long, arduous, and emotionally challenging journey.

My mother's death created a life-altering crisis for me. She was the last in my deaf family for whom I assumed responsibility. I didn't know who I was without being an advocate for the deaf, signing for them, assuaging their fears by taking personal responsibility for their problems, living through the conflicts, and feeling sad because their lives were so *different*.

My parents faced many challenges and in their era (I was born in 1947) where being deaf was totally different than it is today. The 'deafies' as they're now called have much more opportunity to advance themselves via education and technology. Today the deaf have 'Deaf Pride' which is represented by their belief, courage and strength in their unique culture.

After Mom's death there was no one to depend on me (I was divorced and my children were grown). Defining me without the connection to the deaf community was the ultimate conflict for me. Who was I without the responsibility for my family? I unconsciously and consistently defined myself as a caregiver.

Mine is an unusual life as a child of deaf adults. It has been filled with abuse, tremendous responsibility, resentment, sadness, shame and self-actualization. Through all the trials and tribulations, I knew my parents loved me and it was my primary desire to make them happy and life less difficult for them. I had no choice other than to be an excellent communicator and became so at an early age. After Dad's and then Mom's passing, my skills as an interpreter and advocate weren't needed. My fifty-five years of advocacy for my family no longer existed. It was time to cut the intricate strings of dependency. Where do I go from here? That thought was more than frightening.

I came to realize the dependency actually was also mine; I obliviously depended on their needs to define me. With Mom's death it was and continues to be my time to survive as a hearing man in the hearing world. I'll never completely stop being a care giver; that's who I am. I was born a care giver.

I care deeply about people; especially those with emotional and physical challenges. But, I had to consciously transition away from my personal journey of silence to experience the freedom I needed from the mental ties and victimization of my own dependency that bound me. For some people, when the need for care giving ceases, for whatever reason, the emotional ties don't end immediately. In my case, the years of care giving ended abruptly and without warning. The evolving process of emotional separation and self-discovery was hard and confusing, to say the least.

The emotional freedom from caring for others is a process and it's filled with a plethora of feelings. It takes determination, the will to survive in a new and different way, and the ability to live in the present moment without looking into the rear view mirror of the past. I attest that it can be done. I did it.

Talking Hands

I can talk with my hands, can you?

My fingers move in beautiful sign.

Fast or slow, it's so beautiful to do.

Who says you must talk with your voice?

For those are many who cannot.

They were not born with that choice.

So, when you see people talking in sign

They're probably deaf; so special they are.

It's no joke and neither mime.

Benson David…from the book "Survivor of Silence"

I Can Hear With My Eyes

I see differently than you.

The colorful lights, the smiling babies.

The expressions on your faces…

Are definitely not "maybes."

It is the "eye" who is deaf.

And my eyes are my ears.

If I were to lose them.

I'd shed many tears!

The colors of life and everyday sounds.

Are channeled through as they abound.

Just how many tries can you try?

Can you hear with your eyes like I?

Benson David Evans…from the book "Survivor of Silence"

The Dedication of Love

A Tribute To My Deaf Parents.

The dedication of love doesn't end with death.

And, it doesn't end with a loved-one's last breath.

When do you think it is severed?

Can you answer that question?

In my opinion, the answer is never, not ever.

The dedication of love doesn't change with time

As pure as the beautiful white dove,

It's in our hearts, forever, this dedication of love.

Benson David Evans...from the book "Survivor of Silence"

LIFE

Life is like a playground
Sometimes it is flat and sometimes very mountainous.

There may be crashing sounds or silence.
Lives filled with serious matters or sometimes
humorous.

It is said our lives are planned
By a Force far greater than we.
I believe this to be true.
So many peaks and valleys we could never foresee.

The lives of our past mingle with the present.
Then so quickly slip through our fingers.
Hopefully, with joy we can project the present from
the past.
And, when we pass our soul does not linger.

Life is an enigma to many of us.
With questions infinite and answers few.
If FAITH is our walking partner through our life's path,
Than footsteps of our lives are blessed with truth.

Benson David Evans…from the book "Survivor of
Silence"

xx

CHAPTER ONE

LOSING MOTHER

There she was, Nettie, my mother, the woman I so loved and cared for, lying in the sterile-looking hospital bed with flowered sheets she loved. She was under the care of hospice to make her passing as comfortable as possible. The steel bed was strategically placed in the middle of the living room of Mom's condo and at the head of it there was an oxygen tank with its plastic tubes connected to Mom's nose. Pictures of the family and the Get Well cards and flowers from family and friends surrounded her. Mother was dying. Smoking would finally do her in from lung cancer. The addiction that was to her a pleasurable activity would end her life. She had been a long time smoker although she says she never inhaled...I knew better.

My mother, Nettie, was a woman of great fortitude, a New Englander with quite a staunch constitution. Like many Bostonians, she was not one to show her vulnerability or emotion. And now, here she lay in the most vulnerable challenge of her life. I'll never forget the final Thursday of her life as I watched Mother peacefully sleeping. Her worn and wrinkled hands were moving in undistinguishable sign. It was then I realized that she was dreaming and her communication in the dream was expressed through the sign language of the deaf. It was one of the most poignant moments of life for me. To a deaf person hands are the mouth and voice through which they communicate. Hands can have a language of their own.

That night my sister, Myra, and I were sitting on either side of Mom's bed. This was the only time I wished I couldn't hear because the sounds of Mother's labored breathing were awful. There were intermittent gasps, long periods of no breath, and sounds I knew were not good. Then it happened…the lights started flickering. At first I thought it was a momentary power outage. After looking out the window and seeing that no one else's lights were flickering I felt Mom's spirit leave. It had left for her next journey. I had always had strong intuitive abilities and this feeling was overwhelmingly eerie.

The next day, Barbara, the compassionate hospice nurse, arrived at nine in the morning and examined Mother. Mother had no blood pressure and a very faint pulse. Barbara explained that death was imminent. Although we knew death was imminent I just didn't feel prepared for Mom's passing. Myra and I hovered over Mother with intense and fearful focus. Neither of us had been present at anyone's death. A few hours later Mother's breathing became increasingly labored and Myra took one of Mom's hands and I the other and we held them tight. It was as though they were the umbilical cord responsible for our lives. The warmth of her hand comforted me. She pursed her lips then breathed her last breath. One moment later her hands no longer moved. The hands that were her voice were painfully silent. I stared at those hands for what seemed an eternity. At one o'clock February 2, 2001 our mother, Nettie Garfinkle died. It was that day my life as I had known it for fifty-five years died with her.

It was only six weeks previous Mother had not felt well saying that her back hurt and she was having difficulty walking. Within five days of telling me of her pain her condition led to a paralysis from the waist down. Previous to her sudden paralysis I took her to the doctor who examined her thoroughly.

He asked me her age. When I told him she was eighty-seven, he was astonished. He said she was an attractive woman who looked like she was in her late fifties. Mother liked that statement; she had read the doctor's lips. But, when we left the doctor's office, Mother scolded me for telling the doctor her age. She had read my lips, too. Her age was something she never liked discussed.

The doctor ordered a chest x-ray which results showed a large mass in her left lung. He wanted a more in-depth picture and ordered and scheduled a CAT scan. A few days after her visit with the doctor and prior to the day of her CAT scan, Mother's condition worsened and I rushed her to the hospital. After extensive testing and the CAT scan the diagnosis of a mass in her right lung was confirmed. In addition, a mass was found in her liver and a liver biopsy was scheduled to determine the pathology of the tumor.

The next day I tearfully and emotionally watched Mother wheeled into the operating room. About an hour later, the operating room doors opened with Mom on the gurney. The physical pain she endured because of the procedure was obvious and conveyed by her contorted facial expressions and tears in her eyes. Watching her suffer felt like a serrated knife had gone through my heart!

"DEAF-CANNOT SPEAK" was the handwritten sign one of the nurses in the hospital placed over her bed. Mother was horrified and angry at the sight of this sign. She didn't like to be defined (only) as a deaf person. She was embarrassed. Embarrassment became part of her because of her own mother's shame about her daughters' deafness and a society that ridiculed people who were *different*. There was no equality for the deaf.

Truthfully, Mother did not like being deaf. She never had the sense of pride about herself that the deaf have today.

Later that night, the oncologist on staff asked to speak with Myra and me. Our meeting was held in a typical hospital conference room. The room lacked warmth – it was cold and sterile looking a reflection not dissimilar from that of the oncologist himself. I didn't want to be in this room. The doctor said he had 'good news and bad news.' I asked that he give us the bad news first. "Your mother has small cell lung cancer; it is the most virulent type of lung cancer one could have." Then he added that "the good news is with chemotherapy she could last, perhaps, one more year and have a very easy death." I asked what would happen if we chose not to choose the chemotherapy option. Bluntly, he said she would have a very difficult and painful death. Of course, the chemo would make her sick, she'd lose her hair (Mother was very vain) and she would still be paralyzed due to a compressed spine caused by a malignant tumor spun off from the one in the lung. It took only seconds for us to decide against the chemotherapy route.

We told the doctor chemotherapy was not an option. The doctor was furious and asked me what right I had to withhold treatment. I told him "I am her son and this is the most loving act I can make". To this day I'll never forget his cold, callous, judgmental and abrasive reaction. His guilt-provoking words remained with me for many years. There was no warm and caring bedside manner; just the cold facts and judgment, period.

Myra and I decided not to tell Mother the diagnosis and prognosis and did our best to make her comfortable in her own home.

She was released from the hospital and brought home in an ambulance. We arranged twenty four hour care for her. We wanted to make her end of life one of quality. There were many visits from family and friends and all were welcomed by her. I'll never forget her three year old great-granddaughter, Emily, walking next to her in the wheelchair gazing up at her. Mother had never met her because she lived in another state. Emily held one of Mom's hands in hers while I pushed the wheelchair. I had to choke back tears at this unforgettable moment.

After one of her visits, Barbara, (the hospice nurse) asked to speak with me. Her face expressed the seriousness and nature of the issue. She said my mother wanted to know about her condition and wanted to know why she wasn't being told what was wrong with her. Barbara said I needed to be truthful and give Mother the facts about her medical condition. I've never had to tell anyone they were dying. I went to Mother's bed and she looked directly into my eyes and made the sign for 'wrong' wanting to know what was wrong. I said "Mother, you have a tumor in your lung and it is cancerous. We can talk about chemo if you want". Her response was, 'It doesn't help'. Then she said that whatever God wanted she would accept. Although she wasn't religious, she did believe in a higher power.

What she said after that took me by surprise and I held back my tears. She said she was worried about *me*. I asked why and she said "Ben, you are alone". I replied "Well, Mother, you have been alone, a widow, for thirty years and you've managed. I think I can handle it." I said. That statement wasn't true. I was deluding myself. I was unaware of the difficult time that lay ahead for me. Mother's concern for my well-being overwhelmed me. After all the years of caring for her, being her ears and voice, she was now concerned for me.

WOW. That was an unusual feeling. It was one of few times I viewed her as my mother not a dependant for whom I was responsible; like a child for whom I would make decisions.

RESPONSIBLE*: "Liable to be required to give account, as of one's actions or of the discharge of a duty or trust."* This is a word and definition rooted in my core. I was too young to have such adult responsibility, but I had no choice. Responsibility for my family became the purpose of my life and defined who I was and am today. What does it feel like to have another's well-being within one's power? I know very well. Yet, in truth, I had no accountability for myself. I didn't know or feel the 'real' me. The world of "silence" that defined my life had total control over me. It was only as my Mother lay dying did I understand the real implications of my childhood, the loss of my own voice; a voice lost in the silent world.

Sometimes the outcome of the fear we feel can actually be for our benefit. I was always afraid of making the wrong decisions for my family. But, I am grateful for the experience because I learned how to make sound decisions, assume responsibility, and do what had to be done. Just like the Nike slogan, "Just Do It", I'm a 'doer'. I just did what *had* to be done.

CHAPTER TWO

OUR HERITAGE

I'm nine years old sitting on a chair next to "Ma", my maternal grandmother, Esther Weiss. We're sitting on the front porch of our house in Union, NJ, surrounded by the then in-style jalousie windows, the kind you crank to open and close them. It's a warm sticky summer day and Ma is sitting in an aluminum framed woven beach chair. Her soulful dark eyes look intently into the past as I ask her to tell me about the 'old country'. Her short bobbed silver-gray hair is neatly combed off her face and she's dressed in a finely pressed floral housedress with a hankie in her hand. She was never without a clean white hankie. She was a strong stout woman about five feet tall with a distinct erect posture. Her feet are cloaked in what I remember as big clunky black leather shoes that tied, like the ones Nuns wear. The heels weren't very high, about two inches, but they were thick. These shoes were called "Wide Side Kid" shoes made by Coward. She used to take me into New York City every six months to buy a new pair. We had a great time there window shopping and having lunch at the famous and now defunct Horn & Hardart Cafeteria. I'll never forget the formidable sound the shoes made as she walked up and down the uncarpeted stairs **clunk, clunk, clunk.** Her face is majestic with a slender nose that turned up and high check bones. The beauty she

9

had as a young woman still shined through. She was hardly wrinkled but I could see and feel the challenges and sadness of her life etched on her face.

One of her favorite pass times was sitting on the porch watching the cars drive by our house. There were only four houses on our street and it was situated between two major streets. Because of its location between the two major streets, Vauxhall Road and Morris Avenue, it was used as a shortcut. She knew just about every make of car that passed. Memorizing the make and model of cars kept her mind stimulated. I was always amazed at her memory. And when a two-door car passed she felt sorry for the driver saying it was a shame they couldn't afford a four door car (she could never quite comprehend that a two door car was a sports model).

The way she told her stories with her Russian accent made me feel I was actually living in that time and place in the Ukraine. Ma was born in a rural community outside of Kiev in the Ukraine called Alexandrovska. She was one of twelve children born to Fanny and Joseph Futoronsky. (Franklin was later the name given to them when they arrived at Ellis Island). Unfortunately, their first four children died from Diphtheria as infants or toddlers. Ma was the first child to survive. Thereafter, every two years Fanny would give birth to another child. She had seven more healthy children who, somehow, avoided the plague.

Ma had many chores including taking the chickens they raised to the slaughter house. By

Jewish law the chicken had to be slaughtered in compliance of the law with its jugular vein slashed and a Rabbi in attendance to ensure the proper ritual. Cutting the animal's jugular vein is done so the animal feels no pain. Jewish law prohibits eating the meat of an animal that died in pain. Going to the slaughter house was not one of her favorite chores, but she did what her mother told her. Esther's other chores included cooking, gathering the hens' eggs and washing clothes. It was a way of life so different from mine; so foreign and so simple. I was completely intrigued and immersed in listening to her stories.

Esther's mom, Fanny, was a short rotund woman who wore a babushka on her head. Esther's dad, Joseph, was tall, about six feet, dark and handsome. Ma would always be so proud when she told anyone his height. Being six feet tall in our family was truly a gift from God! [We're a family of short people]. In their village, Joseph was known as one of the most talented and well-known designers of women's clothes; especially coats.

The Futoronskys were well-known in their schtetel (village) and recognized as kind, warm-hearted people who always extended a loving hand to anyone in need. There was always someone invited to share dinner. It was an honor to have guests share with their family. Their house always abounded with food including fresh chickens, geese, fresh goat's milk and all the wonderful tasty ethnic kosher delicacies that Fanny cooked or baked. She was an excellent cook making her own pickles and pickled herring and well-known for her baking. Anyone growing up Jewish would really appreciate her culinary talents! The delightful blend of aromas called to the people in the community and they automatically knew it was Fanny's cooking.

The winters in this tiny Ukranian community were bitter cold. But, the Futoronsky children always had warm, well-made coats designed and made by Joseph. The four Futoronsky sons learned their father's skills which later became an integral part of their own success.

The three daughters learned how to cook, clean, and sew from their mother and developed a good understanding what it meant to be a "good wife".

Family life for the Futoronskys was comfortable and happy in spite of the political climate of the era. It was very difficult for a Jewish family living in the Ukraine because antisemitism and many restrictions and pogroms were very prevalent. Daily life and safety were becoming increasingly unpredictable.

Ma had a first cousin by the name of Morris Wisokowsky (later changed to Weiss). He was Fanny's sister's son. Morris lived in the same community as the Futoronskys. Morris and Esther were very close as children and often played together. Their fondness for each other blossomed as they approached adolescence and adulthood. It was not unusual for Jewish families, during that era, to arrange marriages for their children. Marriage to first cousins, too, was not an unusual result of the match making. Mother and Father Futoronsky and Mother and Father Wisokowsky felt it would be a good idea to arrange a marriage between Esther and Morris. After all, they were such great friends and so close. They felt they would make a wonderful couple.

Because of the dangerous political climate, Joseph and Fanny talked about coming to America. They were not without concern about leaving their own parents and family. Life for Jews was worsening and decisions had to be made. Fanny had relatives who had immigrated to America and who told them that opportunity and religious tolerance prevailed in this wonderful country. After much discussion and soul searching they made the decision…on to America for the Futoronskys - Joseph, Fanny and their seven children!

Ma described their trip to America as difficult and unpleasant. They were travelling by ship. She said that many people, including her, became seasick and that the sea was ugly green and smelled awful; especially in Liverpool. It wasn't easy for a mother, father, and seven children to embark on this journey. (Their eighth child was born in America). It was a long and suffering trip with many people becoming ill. There was a variety of illnesses including dysentery and flues. Fanny and Joseph insisted there be no complaining and that they be patient. Their goal was to reach America, taste the sweet flavor of freedom and start their new lives. After the long and arduous trip they arrived at Ellis Island, as most immigrants, and from there set their sights on locating in Worcester, MA, where many Jewish immigrants

13

settled in the early 1900s. Fanny had relatives in Worcester who would help them acclimate to their new country.

Esther immediately enrolled in night school to learn English. She was twenty years old and in a country and language totally foreign to her. There were no boundaries in her determination to assimilate the ways of her new country. She was very impressed with people who had the desire to attain and complete their education. Her education in the Ukraine was minimal and she wanted to be an "educated lady".

Morris had settled in Worcester prior to his cousin Esther's arrival. He secured a job, as many Jewish Immigrants had, working as a tailor specializing in the design and manufacture of ladies' coats. He was very successful and eventually opened up his own factory. A sign of success was his driving around town in his newly purchased black Buick automobile. He was the talk of the town!

The arranged engagement of marriage to Morris was no surprise. Esther and Morris's parents had already made the decision for them. Since they were in love, anyway, there was no resistance by either of these two young people. Everyone was pleased and the wedding date was set.

It is a Jewish custom that the groom smashes with his foot the glass from which the Rabbi has the wedded couple drink the ceremonial wine. The glass was wrapped in a white cloth napkin and Morris smashed it on the first try! (It took me three tries at my

14

own wedding) Morris and Esther were now Mr & Mrs. Weiss. As any couple would, they experienced joy and bliss at their joining together and in what they hoped a long and successful life.

Esther was content and comfortable in her role as a wife. She had learned so much from her mother about being a good wife that she now used in her own life. She became well-known as a great cook and busied herself with her many "wifely tasks". Morris was very proud of his wife. He was very busy with the challenges of a burgeoning enterprise. Since business was booming, he made room for all of Esther's brothers in his business with positions of importance. In Worcester he was known a good and kind man with excellent business sense.

CHAPTER THREE

SOMETIMES PRAYERS ARE NOT ANSWERED THE WAY WE HOPE

One of the most beautiful and exciting times in life is when a couple learns they are expecting a baby. This was no different for Esther and Morris. Esther was a woman who adored children and who wanted twelve. I can remember her broad smile whenever she saw a child in a carriage or stroller. She beamed a smile of true love and affection for the smallest and innocent of God's human creatures.

When most couples are pregnant they hope their child will be born with ten fingers, ten toes, and healthy. This was no different for Esther and Morris who joyously anticipated the arrival of their first child.

After an uneventful pregnancy, on January 15, 1910, their first daughter, Eva, was born. She was a beauty with jet black hair and porcelain white skin. She had the ten fingers, ten toes, and appeared in great health. All was well and the proud parents doted on their new addition. The joy of becoming parents obliterated any thought that there might be something wrong with her. When Eva was about the age of three months, Esther intuitively felt something wasn't right. Her baby didn't respond to noise or her voice. She would just have a blank stare when they made a noise to see if she could hear. Feeling anxious, she decided to bring Eva to their physician.

During his examination the doctor determined Eva was born deaf. Esther and Morris were devastated hearing this. It couldn't be! She seemed like a perfect baby from the moment she was born. When asked what may have been the cause, the doctor replied that marriages between cousins, especially first cousins, are risky. He said that it was not uncommon for the offspring of first cousin marriages to be either blind, deaf, mentally challenged or all of the above. On the other hand, he said that some offspring of cousin marriages can be exceptionally talented children. Today the statistics are that there is a 3-4 percent chance of a physical abnormality to a child of inter-cousin unions. Whether or not there is going to be a child with a defect is contingent upon how many and what defective genes exist. Although Esther and Morris loved Eva, they (Esther in particular) carried the embarrassment, guilt and shame of having a deaf child. Never in her wildest dreams did she expect any defects in her children. There were no previous children born into either the Franklin or Weiss families with any kind of physical challenges. Imagine…carrying a child in for nine months, giving birth, and then three months later hearing your child is deaf.

Every man and woman who has a child with a disability copes with the challenges differently. The range of emotions can range from confusion, fear, guilt, shame, and denial. On the other hand, some parents respond with loving pride. Esther and Morris loved Eva but knew that life for her would not be the same as theirs; it would be filled with many more challenges and be different.

As Eva grew to be a toddler she brought great joy to her parents. I've been told by many relatives that she was a special girl with dimples and a very bubbly personality. Esther and Morris discussed having more children and pondered this issue seriously. They consulted their physician who indicated the predictability of having another deaf child was all a matter of probability,"a crap shoot". In those days there wasn't anything like the genetic testing we have today. They decided to take their chances and have a playmate for Eva. Their thoughts and hope were that maybe this time the child would be 'normal.' They prayed and prayed. Sometimes prayers are not answered the way we hope.

It was a beautiful fall day in Worcester, MA when on October 26, 1913, my mother, Nettie Weiss was born. She was pretty…but, not as pretty as Eva. She was tinier, too. That didn't matter to Esther since her love for children (especially her own) was so strong. She was not good natured a baby as Eva, either, and required more attention than her sister. Having gone through the discovery of Eva's deafness, Esther and Morris were particularly vigilant in their observation as to whether Nettie was deaf. The unwelcomed lack of response to noise was a definite sign…Nettie was deaf, too.

Eva and Nettie had everything that children could want except for their hearing. Fortunately, Morris's business was a tremendous success and there were no financial worries. The girls were always impeccably dressed and groomed and had the best medical care.

As the two girls grew older Esther and Morris discussed the desire for a proper education for the girls. They decided that their children would attend the private and prestigious Clark School for the Deaf in Northampton, MA. The girls would live there during the week. The school was known for its emphasis on 'oral' communication which refers to the using of a deaf person's verbal skills rather than sign language. Sign language could be used off-campus but was prohibited on campus. Mother told me that she and her best friend and roommate, Gertrude (Gertie) Slotnick, would hide in the bathroom and speak with each other in sign language. When it was dark they would use a flashlight in order to see each other.

Mother was always envious that Gertrude's mother was very supportive of her daughter using sign language to communicate. She was not ashamed of her daughter either. On the other hand, Esther did not approve of her daughters' use of sign language. If the teachers at Clark said this was the preferred way of teaching the deaf, that was the gospel for Esther. To this day I feel prohibiting the use of sign language resulted in difficulty for the deaf in communicating with their deaf peers who were taught sign language. Mother was never fluent and always relied on others who knew the language to assist. Most of the time she would read the lips of both the deaf and hearing. Her verbal skills were rather minimal. She had a screechy voice and tried hard to achieve the correct pronunciation of words and the correlating sounds. For most 'normal' people it would have been almost impossible to understand her. Thank goodness that in today's contemporary deaf culture and education sign language is the acceptable and preferred mode of communication. ASL (American Sign Language) is recognized as a language in its own right. I rank it as one of the most beautiful languages in existence. ASL is taught in colleges and universities across the country.

Eva and Nettie were two happy children and approached adolescence with the same excitement that any normal adolescent would. Although they were very close to each other they both had friends in their own individual social circle. Nettie looked up to her older sister Eva as a role model and had tremendous admiration for her. They enjoyed a very special sisterhood and friendship.

They devotedly relied on each other. Eva was a teacher to Nettie who learned about living as a deaf person from her. Eva was an exceptional example of how a young deaf girl could be happy in a hearing world; she was content with whom she was.

Life doesn't always turn out as we want. Eva was thirteen and Nettie ten when their dad, Morris, became ill. Morris was a slight man of about 5 feet and a thin build. He was a smoker and developed a nagging hacking cough that couldn't be cured by Esther's chicken soup. After much cajoling, Esther insisted he see a doctor. The doctor said he needed x-rays to determine the cause. The outcome was one that no one wanted or expected. Morris had cancer. He was only thirty seven years old, a devoted husband, dad, and a successful businessman. Esther's life would forever change. She dedicated herself to caring for the husband she loved and adored. Although there were many challenges facing her in the care of her husband, caring for him was easy because of her great love for him.

Eva and Nettie were away at school for the major portion of their father's illness. They came home to visit him on weekends and holidays. As the end of Morris's life approached, the girls were summoned home. They knew he was ill and missed him but Esther wanted them to remain in school and not disrupt their education. She wanted her girls to have the best opportunity in life and education was the route that would help provide them a good foundation.

It was a sweltering day on June 30, 1923. With the girls by Esther's side next to Morris's bed he peacefully passed away. Esther was relieved that his two year ordeal was over and he would no longer suffer. Her relief didn't mask her grief though. She lost her beloved life partner. His young life was over at the age of thirty nine. He was too young, too successful, and too good to die. Nevertheless, Esther was now a widow at thirty seven.

Esther, Eva, and Nettie huddled together sobbing…where would life lead them without their husband and dad? He was their provider, their rock, their hope. Life wasn't supposed to be this way.

The next morning the plain pine casket with Morris's body was brought to the home from the mortuary. It was placed in the middle of the living room. People came to pay their respects and brought the customary foods and flowers. Nettie thought one bouquet of roses was particularly beautiful. She bent down and placed her nose to smell the sweet aroma of one. Unknown to her a busy bee was deep within this rose doing his chores. She disrupted him and he stung her right on the nose. It was, indeed, a painful day for Nettie.

Workmen's Circle Cemetery in Worcester, MA sits perched on a hill on the outskirts of the city. Morris's casket was surrounded by hundreds of mourners wearing yarmulkes (skullcaps) and reciting the traditional Jewish Prayers for the dead. Morris was laid to his eternal rest. Also laid to rest was Esther's dream of a long life with her husband. It's been said that life can change in a moment and it did for her.

After the traditional Jewish Shiva (period of mourning) the girls returned to school while Esther tried to determine the direction of their lives. Although Esther was an emotionally strong woman her family and friends couldn't help feel her pain and sadness.

She was alone and responsible for her deaf children and herself.

With Morris's passing, Esther's brothers took control of the business he worked so hard to make a success. For a while things were fine. During the late 1920's, however, business started to slide. Not one of the successor brothers- in-law could manage as Morris had. Esther's brothers, the men she trusted, told her the business needed an infusion of money to keep it going. Esther willingly invested ten thousand dollars. This is about all she had left after the financial drain of Morris's illness. At that time that amount was a whole lot of money! The financial infusion wasn't working. Esther was rapidly losing the income from the business that previously provided her family financial security. As the business failed the ten thousand dollar investment was lost.

Determined to support herself and daughters she went to work. It wasn't uncommon for Jewish immigrant women to work as a seamstress. The factories were basically sweatshops. Esther, who had been accustomed to living a fine life as the wife of a successful businessman, was reduced working in the sweatshop. She didn't complain; there was no choice; so why complain?

Esther had a younger sister Sarah. She was next in the family lineage after Esther. The sisters were very close and adored each other, very much like Eva and Nettie. Sarah had a sense of humor that wouldn't quit and people loved her. She was also very generous. Sarah was married to Jack Weiss a successful owner of a 'dry goods' store in Boston. Jack was also the second cousin of Sarah. They had two boys who were not deaf. Marrying a second cousin wasn't as genetically risky as marrying a first.

24

They had a sprawling two story home in Boston. Much like her mother Fanny, Sarah always had a bevy of friends and family enthusiastically eating Sarah's delicious meals. She was what in Yiddish is known and pronounced as a 'ballabuster' which translates into one great housewife! Jack was not as generous. Sarah would take her nieces; Eva and Nettie, into the store and when Jack wasn't looking give them a stash of 'goodies' and money. She was guardian angel to them. [Later in life when Mother had emergency gallbladder surgery Sarah sent five thousand dollars to help cover medical costs]. She was special to all who had the opportunity to know her.

Esther never complained about her worsening financial circumstances. She couldn't hide her feelings from Sarah and Sarah knew that the loss of Morris and her children being away at school was both financially and emotionally challenging for Esther. After months of pleading, Sarah convinced Esther to sell her home, leave her job, and move from Worcester to Boston to live with her and her family. The tuition for the girls' private education was taking its financial toll. Esther made the decision to withdraw the girls from The Clark School for the Deaf and enroll them in public school. There was a public high school in Boston that had a deaf education curriculum. Aware of their mother's financial challenges, Eva and Nettie agreed to leave although they would have preferred to remain at Clark.

Esther was determined to continue to provide for her family and secured another job in a Boston factory as a seamstress. No longer did she own a home; no longer was there a fancy Buick at her disposal or husband on whom to depend. But, she made her life work for her and her daughters.

The girls sorely missed their dad. They believed in ghosts and often said they felt their dad's presence. With the absence of one sense others become keener. Both Nettie and Eva were clairvoyant and would often see visions.

One story Mom told me is about an experience she and Eva had as they walked home from a party late one night. It was dark and they were anxious to get home. There were trolley tracks and as they stepped onto the tracks the bright light of the trolley was upon them. They had not heard the warning horn. Immediately they felt a force grab them by their collars and pull them away from being severely injured or killed. Until the day she passed Nettie was convinced it was her father who had saved their lives.

As the girls grew out of adolescence into young womanhood they grew even closer and were almost inseparable. They studied hard in school and both graduated from public high school and secured factory jobs. Securing a job in a factory sewing or assembling products was about all that a deaf young woman could get in those days.

CHAPTER FOUR

EVA: DREAMS MADE, DREAMS DIED

Beautiful, vivacious, funny, gregarious, and a *'good voice'* are all adjectives that were used to describe my Aunt Eva. It's common among the deaf to want to know if a deaf person has a good voice. Mother would always ask me that question about her friends or a new deaf person she met. It was as though there were some kind of competition for the best voice!

Attracting young men was not a challenge for Eva. There were many suitors and one in particular caught her eye. He was tall, handsome, smart and deaf. His name was Samuel. All the girls wanted him, too, but Eva was the fortunate one. Samuel and Eva dated steadily for about one year and Nettie was very happy for Eva. Nettie, herself, had not much desire to find a man.

The engagement was no surprise to anyone. Eva glowed with joy and was happier than she could ever dream. Esther was thrilled and bought her a Hope Chest. A Hope Chest was a piece of furniture in which a betrothed would store items to be used after the wedding. There were gifts of china, flatware, sheets, lingerie and more in the chest and Eva excitedly prepared for her wedding.

Her friend Etta Weinstein was unhappy about losing Eva's attention. She and Eva had been friends for years and her fear of their friendship changing with the impending marriage grew. She designed a scheme to prevent the marriage.

She started by convincing Eva she needed a diversion from planning the wedding. She explained that too much attention to one thing was not good. Always up for a party Etta arranged for her and Eva to attend as many parties as could be found.

Unbeknownst to Eva, Etta was telling Samuel that Eva was having 'too much fun' and that Eva was dating other men. Samuel believed Etta and Immediately and unconditionally broke the engagement. To say Eva was devastated is an understatement. Her usual happy-go-lucky personality turned morose. She felt she had no purpose to life; that the love of her life was lost, and life was not good to her. Nettie's attempts to help her older sister out of her depression met with futility. Eva never discovered the ploy architected by Etta. Samuel told Eva he didn't trust her and he the engagement was done. Eva's life force slowly ebbed away.

Boston is well known for its cold winters and the one of nineteen hundred and thirty three was no different. Eva developed a bronchial infection which worsened rapidly and seriously alarmed Esther. Esther and Nettie tried to talk Eva into going to a doctor but she refused. Her cough was horrific and her condition seriously deteriorated. After coming home from work Eva went to bed. This was very unusual for this once very energetic young woman. Checking on her later that evening, Esther discovered she was breathing laboriously and immediately called the doctor for help. Nettie sat intensely by her sister, her best friend, her companion in silence. Holding Nettie's hand, Eva's last words to her were that she welcomed death and to please bury her in her Hope Chest. With Esther and Nettie by her side Eva gasped, blood gushed from her nose and mouth, and she died. When the doctor arrived it was too late. The only thing he could do was to pronounce her dead. Her death certificate was to read the cause of death was "Walking Pneumonia"; it should have said "Broken Heart". Maneuvering through the silence Nettie had known would never be the same without her beloved sister, best friend, and partner in silence.

A parent's nightmare is to bury their child. This was the case for Esther. Jewish Law is that the dead be buried within twenty four hours. January sixteenth, nineteen hundred thirty three, was cold and dreary. Mourners came from far and near to B'nai Brith Cemetery in Worcester the same cemetery on the hill where Eva's dad, Morris, rested. There were classmates from both Clark and the Public High Schools Eva attended. Family, friends, and neighbors sat as the Rabbi read the prayers for the soul of this beautiful young being. As the casket was lowered into the open grave Esther bolted and tried to throw herself on it. She screamed that she wanted to be buried with her daughter. Esther had hoped her oldest daughter would have a happy, long and good life. It wasn't meant to be. Some dreams are made and then die.

The grief over this tragic loss was almost unbearable for Nettie. Although she returned to work, her grief was overwhelming. She suffered from anxiety, confusion and anorexia. She lost significant weight and cried most of the time. Esther, dealing with her own grief, was alarmed for Nettie's well-being.

She literally dragged her to the doctor's office. The doctor warned Nettie that her health was in jeopardy and prescribed medication and vitamins to build her strength. He talked with her in a kind and compassionate way saying that although it is ok to grieve, she should move forward and live her life the best she could. Nettie read his lips and understood. She tried her best but life was never the same without Eva.

Esther, too, was never the same. Life brought her much sadness. Although she could laugh; joke, and smile, the hint of melancholy permeated her being. Sarah told Esther the best thing for her to do was to return to work and occupy her mind. Esther always listened to her younger sister and returned to her job. But, she now had one more purpose. That purpose was to ensure Nettie's well-being and happiness. To Esther happiness was finding a good man, making him happy, and having children. Nettie was uninterested.

Nettie's grief was lessened by eating and, at four ten and a half, Nettie became slightly plump which was fashionable in those days. She had an olive complexion with jet black hair and her black eyes, as most deaf people's are, were very expressive. She had a close knit circle of a few good friends, including Gertrude (Gertie) her roommate at Clark. They liked to go to friends' parties, the movies (which were not captioned at the time) and the dance hall. There were men interested dancing with Nettie and she gladly accepted. She and her dancing partner would dance to the beat of the vibration from the music. A night out with a man was fine for her but any serious dating was rebuffed. Perhaps her resistance to a serious relationship was clouded by the tragic outcome of her sister's. For Nettie, life was good just the way it was; no need to change it. She liked her family, friends, her job and that was perfect for her.

CHAPTER FIVE

ANOTHER ARRANGED MARRIAGE

Life was consistent for Nettie and that's the way she liked it. She worked, attended deaf functions, and Esther taught her how to crochet, knit and sew. Hand crafts were peaceful activities for her and helped divert her mind from mundane daily activities and especially the loss of her sister.

Although Esther loved having her daughter with her she wanted her to have a family life of her own. One by one Nettie's girlfriends, including Gertie, were marrying. The opportunity to be a career woman, especially for a deaf woman was not as they are today. Marriage then would provide a woman with financial security.

Esther wanted Nettie to marry. She felt it was the best option to provide her with stability. She asked Nettie's deaf girlfriends to help convince Nettie that finding a good man and raising a family is what a woman *should* do. She didn't view spinsterhood favorably for her daughter.

Esther and Nettie had moved into their own flat in Dorchester, MA leaving the security of Sister Sarah's home. Needing extra money to support herself and Nettie, Esther brought in a 'border'. Today a 'border' would be called a roommate. The border was an older widow woman, Mrs. Kaplan. Coincidentally Mrs. Kaplan had a friend in Newark,

33

NJ, whose son was deaf. His name was Max Garfinkle. He was thirty two years of age and came from a very good family. He even had his own business which was unusual for a deaf person in those days. He owned the newsstand on the corner of Market and Broad Streets in downtown Newark. Everyone in town knew of Max and his broad, 'happy to see you' smile. The 'Newark Star-Ledger', the regional newspaper even wrote an article and picture of him as a favorite local attraction. The wheels turned and turned in Esther's mind. She wanted these two people, with their common challenges, to meet. Mrs. Kaplan was asked to do a 'mitzvah' which in Hebrew means 'blessing.'

Coincidentally, Nettie and Max were both members of 'The Frat' a social organization for the deaf. Max was the President of his local chapter in Newark and very well respected. He was gregarious, charismatic, and a natural leader unlike Nettie who tended to be introverted. Max, unlike Nettie, never mourned the loss of his hearing [except once to say he wished he could hear his childrens' voices].

Mrs. Kaplan knew Max was single. His engagement to a young deaf woman from Long Island, NY recently ended. The woman broke off the relationship. [He must have deeply cared for this woman since he carried her picture in his wallet to the day he died]. Mrs. Kaplan gave her friend Nettie's address and asked that she give it to Max who could, in turn, write to Nettie. And, he did. The correspondence lasted a couple of months with Nettie being unimpressed and indifferent about Max as a prospective husband.

One day Nettie went to the mailbox and there was an envelope containing another letter from Max. She nonchalantly opened it. Max was coming to town! He was coming to Boston to meet with the President of the Frat Chapter in that city and he wanted to finally meet Nettie. Nettie showed the letter to her mother who grinned from ear to ear. Nettie smirked. When Nettie smirked it was with a distinctly disgusted expression especially when she intensely disliked something. There was no doubt you could tell how she felt! Esther firmly insisted that out of kindness and respect she should meet him. Nettie caved in and agreed to meet him.

Nettie met Max on a warm July evening in nineteen hundred thirty five. Max was gracious. Nettie was courteous. They danced and talked. It was an eventful night for Max...for Nettie it was, as she described it, 'alright.' Max asked if Nettie would agree to continue the correspondence, she said yes, and the connection continued.

Predictably, Nettie received another letter. This letter was different; Max wanted her to come to Newark and visit with him and his family. Nervously, she showed the letter to Esther who insisted she accept the invitation. Nettie was usually compliant with Esther's demands and this was no different. When Esther wanted something done she wanted it done right then and there! She could be very domineering. The trip was arranged and Nettie would take the train from Boston to Newark, NJ to visit with Max and his family.

Max had a large family; his parents had six boys and they were all excited about meeting Nettie. The Garfinkles were known as a good Jewish family. They all went to Synagogue on Saturdays, obeyed the Jewish Laws and customs and had successful careers. Nettie was treated like royalty by the family. Tobie, Max's mother immediately bonded with Nettie and felt that she was the daughter she never had. Although Nettie enjoyed the time she spent she didn't have the desire to become involved in a serious relationship. Neither did she care for Newark. Max was more serious than Nettie. Nettie spent the weekend and then happily returned to Boston. She loved Boston, the deaf activities there and the city itself. And importantly Boston was where her family and friends were.

Immediately upon Nettie's departure Tobie phoned Esther to tell her how impressed she was with Nettie and that what a great match these two deaf people would make. Esther agreed. Nettie was still not interested and wanted her life to remain as it was. Max continued to write Nettie and pleaded for her to seriously consider a relationship with him. Nettie was bombarded by both Esther and her friends: "Don't be a spinster", "You'll be sorry", "He comes from a good family", "Make a family of your own" were compelling clichés used to nudge [or rather push] Nettie to make her decision. Listening to her mother and friends, Nettie began to reconsider. There were two more visits with Max prior to his marriage proposal. Nettie reluctantly caved in and said yes. It was a match, a match made similar to how her own mother and father were joined. But, the difference was love. For Nettie there was never love; it was a marriage of convenience. The two deaf people would help and support each other, raise a family, and grow old together as partners in silence.

The courtship was short, six months. The setting for their wedding was a small synagogue in Newark. On January 3, 1936 Nettie and Max were married in the presence of their families and friends. Esther and Max's parents had achieved their goal and they were pleased. After a three day honeymoon in New York City they settled in Newark in a third floor tenement apartment close to Max's parents. Nettie always missed Boston, the city she loved, her friends and Esther who was now alone. Although missing her daughter, Esther was grateful Nettie was not alone; she had a partner in the silent world and the Garfinkle Family would look after them.

CHAPTER SIX

ANOTHER BABY GIRL...DEAF

The December of 1937 Nettie became pregnant. She and Max were pleased and looked forward the arrival of their first child. Like her mother, Nettie had always loved children. She had many younger cousins and her friends had children so she wasn't a stranger to the joy children bring.

Nettie was rather prudish about sex. Although she was glad to be pregnant she tried to hide it by wearing large coats...even in the summer! Max proudly thrust his chest forward like a peacock when telling friends and relatives his wife was pregnant. It didn't take much to make him happy. He was content.

With his wife's pregnancy, the corner of Broad and Market Streets where Max's newspaper stand was an even happier place to be!

After an uneventful pregnancy on September 13, 1938 after twelve hours of labor, Nettie and Max became parents. Myra Eva was born. She was a tiny five pounds thirteen ounces and beautiful. She was named in memory of Nettie's beloved father and sister. In the Jewish tradition it is customary to name a newborn after a deceased person as an honor and to keep their spirit alive.

It was a beautiful day; the sun shone and the new parents beamed with pride. Max handed out the traditional cigars with the pink stork on the wrapper. Excitedly, Esther excitedly left Boston to meet her new granddaughter. She was overwhelmed with pride and joy. After visiting her new grandchild and spending time with Nettie and Max, she was satisfied that all was well and returned to Boston and her job.

In 1938 there were no devices to help a deaf person detect a baby's cry. Today there are so many wonderful devices - lights, vibrating apparatuses, video cameras for the deaf to assist them in the responsibilities of parenthood. Nettie slept with her arm outstretched into the crib with her palm face down on the mattress to detect Myra's cry. She could feel the baby crying by the vibration in her hand. Motherhood agreed with Nettie. She had a purpose; she had a child she loved. Her life was more content than ever with the birth of her daughter.

Max and Nettie had hoped their children would have a 'normal' life. They were thrilled when Myra responded to the banging of pots & pans and to their voices. She was a happy baby growing and reacting to noises like any other infant.

Nettie loved strolling with Myra on nice days. Myra's carriage was stored in the narrow hallway of their apartment. When Nettie wanted to take Myra for a stroll she would first take the carriage down three flights of stairs to the lobby of the building. This was not an easy task but she did it. Then she returned to the apartment for Myra. One day while carrying Myra in her arms walking down the stairs Nettie fell. She frantically checked her daughter for injuries and all seemed well. What a relief!

With the coming weeks Nettie and Max noticed a distinct change in Myra's reaction, or lack thereof, to noise. Their joy quickly turned to sorrow.

Upon taking her to the doctor for examination, he diagnosed her as profoundly deaf. The doctor said her deafness was probably the result of the fall. The probability of the deafness being caused by a genetic defect rather than the fall was slimmer because Max was not born deaf. He did not carry the defective gene for hearing. He had become deaf at the age of two due to the effects of spinal meningitis.

Although saddened by their daughter's deafness, they were determined to help guide her through the world of silence, a world with which they were very familiar.

Myra was a happy child who made many deaf and hearing friends.

The depression hit during the time Myra was a toddler. There was no money to send her to private school as had been done for Nettie. She was enrolled in the Bruce Street School for the Deaf, the same school from which her dad, Max, had graduated. It was a public school and did not have the severe restrictions on using sign language like The Clark School for the Deaf. Sign language was taught as the primary mode of communication between the deaf. Max, with his extensive knowledge of sign language, encouraged and taught his daughter the beautiful language of sign. There was a special bond between this father and daughter.

Deaf Pride was no issue for Myra. This child was completely and unconditionally happy with not hearing as was her dad. But, as is the case in many families, her family wished for her to regain her hearing. George, Max's kind and loving brother, was the advocate for his brother and his family. When Myra was four years of age he decided it was time to have Myra's 'condition' evaluated by the top otolaryngologist in New York City. He insisted on paying the bill. The doctor said Myra had about ten percent hearing in her left ear, the right ear had no hearing, and the doctor suggested she wear a hearing aid in the good ear. Although this wouldn't help recover her hearing it would improve her recognition of sounds and help her to learn to speak better. Most deaf people who are born deaf speak all kinds of tones, screeches, and guttural vocal attempts to enunciate words. This is the result of not being able to hear and identify exactly what the sound is and replicate it. The bottom line is that their enunciation can be profoundly different. Difference in most societies isn't welcomed with open arms. The deaf were often thought of as strange, mentally challenged, scary, ridiculed, and pitied. Pity was never in my parents' repertoire of acceptable perceptions. Most hearing people in those days perceived the deaf as lesser beings, a popular phrase was "deaf and dumb". That thought reminds me of the famous movie "Children of a Lesser God." To me

42

being deaf was something I didn't think of as funny. Watching the deaf conquer the challenges of silence to the best of their abilities was, at minimal, inspirational.

Myra was a smart and happy child but she longed for a baby brother or sister and she kept asking her parents for one. She would prefer a sister but, if it were a brother that would be disappointing but acceptable. Her requests were met with sadness. It appeared she would have no sibling. Her parents were not going to have more children. Nettie desperately wanted more but with the probability of the defective gene for hearing, bringing more deaf children into the world was unacceptable for her. There were to be no more risks.

CHAPTER SEVEN

NO MORE [DEAF] CHILDREN!

It's not unusual for one person to control another. The desire to control comes from fear and fear can provoke a variety of reactions from our ego. We all want our lives and the lives of our loved ones to be joyful with minimal challenges and great outcomes. Attempting to control the outcome either of our own life or that of our loved ones is not uncommon. This was the case for Tobie Garfinkle, Max's mother. Although she loved her first born son, Max, having a deaf son was not joyful for her. Although Max was a good boy her heart ached that he had unfortunately lost his hearing. She was indeed proud that he was motivated to start his own newspaper stand business but deep down there was always sympathy for him. In spite of her maternal concern, she was pleased that he had married Nettie and they had a beautiful daughter. Myra was the apple of her eye and at that time, her only grandchild. But something deeply bothered the new and doting grandmother and it was a **BIG** but; Myra was deaf. Although Myra was apparently born with her hearing, Tobie didn't want to risk the probability of any more deaf grandchildren in her family. Even the slightest chance that Nettie might carry the defective gene was enough for her to prevent additional pregnancies.

Nettie depended on Tobie and respected her position on almost everything. As a deaf person, Nettie never felt equal to those who were hearing. If she hadn't felt so insecure about herself she wouldn't have made the decision not to have any more children based on her mother- in- law's edict.

Tobie was compelling in her contention that Nettie shouldn't have more children. Tobie was very influential over Nettie and Nettie reluctantly agreed. But, she never felt good about the decision. Deep in her heart she wanted and longed for more children. Myra continued to ask for a brother or sister. Nettie loved being a mother. Being a mother fulfilled her and gave purpose to her life. Myra would have to accept being an only child. The finality of the decision made her heart ache.

Dr. Gerstenfeld was the gynecologist/-obstetrician for all the women in the Garfinkle family. Nettie adored him. He was kind, gentle and compassionate. Most of all he was concerned with his patients' well-being; especially Nettie's. He developed a special fondness and patriarchal compassion for her.

Myra was six years old when Nettie visited Dr. Gerstenfeld for her annual checkup. He pronounced her in good health. Curious, he asked her if she had thought of having more children. Nettie sheepishly replied that she wasn't going to have any more. Probing further, the doctor asked the reason. She told him that after serious discussion with her mother-in-law she was advised not to have more. He was indignant and outraged. He was angry that Nettie had made this decision based on another person's opinion. His chagrin was evident in his facial expressions that Nettie read so well. He boldly asked Nettie for her mother-in-law's telephone number.

Shortly thereafter, Tobie received a call from the good doctor. He asked her the reason for talking Nettie and Max out of expanding their family. As she had told Nettie, she told him she was afraid there would be more deaf offspring. It would be too much of heartache for her and her family. Doctor Gerstenfeld told her she had no right to influence them one way or the other. He basically told her 'she had a lot of nerve'. He explained to Tobie that although it was unfortunate Myra was deaf, it didn't mean future children would be. And, even if the child *were* deaf, Myra would have a playmate! Humbled, Tobie pondered his comments.

One week later Tobie visited with Nettie, Max and Myra. She told her son and daughter-in-law that Dr. Gersteneld had called her about how she handled the issue of Max and Nettie having more children. She clearly understood his position, apologized and asked forgiveness. If they were to have more children, she would give them her blessing.

Nettie and Max were excited about the prospect of another child. They proceeded to the process of baby making and Nettie soon learned she was pregnant. Joy filled their house and Myra would soon have the sibling she wanted.

The six Garfinkle brothers, their families, and the matriarch of the Garfinkle family, Tobie, rented a beach house in Asbury Park every summer from June through August. The summers in NJ could be very hot, humid, and oppressive. The summer of 1945 was no different. The beach house had three levels and Nettie and Myra shared a room on the second floor. Max would come for the weekend and join them.

The stairs leading to the second level of the house were long and steep. One afternoon she left the room with Myra to go to the beach. Walking down the stairs Nettie's shoe caught in one of the cracks of the old steps at the top of the flight. Losing her footing Nettie rapidly tumbled from the top of the staircase to the bottom. Regaining her footing she seemed fine and walked with Myra to the beach. After about an hour she felt severe pain and decided to return to the room. She started to hemorrhage and Tobie called for an ambulance. She was almost four months pregnant when she miscarried. The fetus was a girl who was to have been named Beth. Nettie, Max and Myra were heartbroken.

Nettie found it difficult to contain her grief. Upon her visit with Dr. Gerstenfeld to assess her post-miscarriage condition, he said there was no reason why they couldn't try again. They did and did and did. Disappointment came on a monthly basis for seven long months. Then the eighth month was a charm! Pregnant again! Joy and anticipation visited them again.

This pregnancy was very difficult for Nettie who had developed gallstones.

Her nausea, pain, and general discomfort were making her miserable. She persevered as best she could because she really wanted this child. Daily vomiting throughout the nine months was not unusual. Although she didn't have much of an appetite she tried to eat as best she could to ensure the fetus had good nutrition. She would have to wait until the baby was born to have surgery to remove the gallbladder. She called it her nine months of hell.

Nettie's due date was January 23, 1947. It was a bitter cold and snowy day on January 11, 1947. Labor pains started that morning. Max's brother, George, was living with their mother. Max trudged through the snow to his mother's house and asked George if he would drive him and Nettie to the hospital. His loving, dutiful and responsible brother drove them to Beth Israel Hospital in Newark and paced the floor along with Max.

After six hours of hard labor I was born, the son of Max and Nettie, Benson David. They rejoiced at the birth and although Myra was disappointed because she wanted a sister, she finally accepted having a brother. I was told I was quite a handsome baby with a full head of dark brown hair.

My proud parents brought me home and introduced me to Myra who was old enough to help change my diapers, feed me and generally assist our mother. She enjoyed the role of big sister; she was almost nine years my senior.

Our family's joy, however, didn't last long. Within two weeks Nettie's gallbladder condition worsened. Her eyes and skin were jaundiced and the pain in her abdomen was unbearable. She was in an already weakened state due to giving birth but the only option was to have emergency surgery. In 1947 the only way the gallbladder and stones could be removed is by what is called an 'open' procedure. In other words, the abdomen is cut open and the gallbladder and its stones are removed. This kind of surgery back then was very risky. [Tobie later died from the same surgery]. Today this procedure is done laparoscopically by inserting instruments into four small incisions and has less associated risks.

Nettie made it through the procedure just fine. Everyone was relieved and Nettie began her recovery. Three days after the initial surgery and still in the hospital recovering she became severely ill with pain, jaundice and nausea, all too familiar symptoms. After an x-ray of her abdomen the surgeon found one of the gallstones had slipped into the common bile duct between the gallbladder and liver causing her severe symptoms. Again, there was no choice but to perform another emergency procedure. Already weak from giving birth and previous surgery, she was wheeled into the operating room and the procedure started. While her abdomen was open she went into cardiac arrest. It took the operating team five minutes to restart her heart. She was technically dead. The medical team was able to complete the surgery but

Nettie was in a coma and her condition was very critical.

Esther was summoned by Tobie who conveyed the gravity of Nettie's condition. She was told she was needed to come help her son-in-law and granddaughter and care for the new baby. Esther was distraught at the thought of losing her only surviving daughter and stoically tried not to obsess about what might happen. Her family needed her and she would be there-unquestionably.

It was one month before Nettie awakened from the coma. It took another month in the hospital to totally recover. Thankfully, the worst was behind her.

When she arrived home her baby who weighed a mere 5lbs 15 oz. at birth was now a chubby two and a half month old infant with big rosy cheeks. Jewish mothers and grandmothers are known for the importance of food in their children's lives... sometimes feeding them too much! At that time it was thought that making children fat would make them healthy.

CHAPTER EIGHT

LOST CHILDHOOD, LOSS OF BEST FRIEND...

Most children at the age of four have simple chores. They include putting away toys, hanging up clothes and responsibilities parents feel their children should learn at that age. Chores help teach children responsibility. It helps them develop self-esteem, self-confidence, and the need for structure in their lives.

My earliest recollection of my first chore was using the telephone. Ma (Grandma Esther) had a telephone installed in our kitchen. It was black with a dial and quite large. It hung there like a monkey on my back. It was made very clear to me by my grandmother, unconditionally, that I was the lifeline to the hearing world for my parents and Myra. I would *always* have to help them.

I could see and feel the relief of my parents knowing there was a new and effective mode of communication and that I was the catalyst, the intermediary. I was their advocate, their representative.

I can clearly remember feeling overwhelmed. I knew that other children my age didn't have to use the telephone and speak for their parents. They were outside playing, climbing, laughing, making snowmen and, in general, just having fun. There was rarely a day that went by when I wasn't called into the apartment to make phone calls, ask a neighbor for help or make adult decisions. Although I knew there was a difference between me and other children, I still in some way felt mine was a 'normal' childhood. That was until I learned I was different. I didn't know I was *different*.

As I grew, the differences between me and other children and my family and other families was more evident and became very clear when I was enrolled in Kindergarten. I attended Hawthorne Elementary School on the corner of Hawthorne and Clinton Avenues in Newark just one block from our tenement apartment on 1 Wolcott Street. When Mom walked me to school and a schoolmate would say 'hi' to her he/she would immediately know there was something different. Mom's voice was of high pitched and screeching in nature. "What's wrong with your mom?" "Why can't she talk?" Sometimes there was a laugh, a snicker, a look of disbelief. I had to repeat the same old thing, "My mom's deaf". "Is your father deaf"? "What – you have a deaf sister, too"! This type of discussion became old- fast.

Not only did my classmates and peers ask questions but those same questions were asked by adults. When the adults asked the questions I felt even more different. Shouldn't they know about deaf people? Hadn't they known what sign language was? [It's always amazed me that the average person doesn't look outside of themselves, their own culture and their own families to recognize there are people who are just not the same as they]. This is all too

54

evident in the lack of knowledge displayed by some people of one religion of the differences of another. Aside from the constant and sometimes foolish questions asked about how I *talked* with my parents, school was pleasurable. I was very bright and precocious and, as one could imagine, quite mature. Yet, one part of me was mature while the other longed to be a carefree child. Parent-teacher conferences were difficult for me. My parents wouldn't attend most of them. They said they couldn't understand what the teacher was saying. As I entered the higher grades I begged them to go and write notes to the teacher and have the teacher write notes about my progress in school. Mom, in particular, went reluctantly. Her timidity and insecurity was noticeably evident.

As I progressed to the second grade Myra was already into her adolescence. Her being deaf integrated into the family better than my integration as a hearing son. Expectations of her were different. She used sign language freely and developed excellent self-perception. She didn't have to answer questions about her parents' deafness because she, too, was deaf. It was different for me. Always questions, questions, curiosity and more curiosity. Myra's circle of friends, although mostly deaf, included some hearing girls and they all seemed to get along and communicate just fine. Myra was stronger than I, less sensitive. There were times I would go to my room, sit in the corner with the door closed and cry because I wanted to have 'normal' parents.

I wasn't without close friends, though. My closest friend was Georgie Krugman, the adopted son of a pharmacist and his wife. The pharmacy was on the corner of Wolcott Terrace and Hawthorne Avenue diagonally across the street from our first floor tenement apartment. His parents were helpful in teaching him about deafness and encouraged his friendship with me. There were other parents who preferred their children not be friends with me…as if deafness were catching. Georgie was a handsome blonde blue-eyed boy with just the most fantastic and loving personality. We were like twin brothers.

Harvey Silverstein was my other close friend. He lived across the street from me in another three story tenement building. I enjoyed his friendship and he never had much curiosity about my family. I preferred it that way. I hated answering all those stupid questions about how deaf people "do this and that."

Living in the tenement apartment was fun. I knew almost all of the tenants and most were very friendly and helpful. Mrs. Marias, an elderly blind woman, lived on the second floor. Ma (Grandma Esther) checked on her every day. She had such compassion and concern for others. Mrs. Marias used to tease me and I am ashamed to admit that I replied with "drop-dead"! That seemed to be the operative phrase for me in those days. One day she was found dead in her apartment and boy did I feel crummy!

There were the Samarins, a wonderful German couple with three lovely young adult daughters. I was always there visiting them in their third floor apartment. Mrs. Samarin was like a second mother to me. I especially looked forward to Christmas in their home every year. I loved helping to decorate the Christmas tree. Being Jewish we did not have one. But, I was permitted to help them and became a great Christmas tree decorator!

I was in second grade when I learned more about the concept of difference and its relationship to discrimination. There was a building maintenance man, Louis. He was black and a man with humor and great Integrity. My Grandmother Esther had a standing luncheon date with him every Wednesday at our home. She loved his stories. One day a few neighborhood women arrived at our apartment. They told my grandmother she should be careful with whom she associated, you know…after all, Louis was a "Negro." Highly offended, my Grandmother told them she would rather have lunch with him any day than lunch with them! I was so proud of her. It was that incident and how my grandmother handled it that taught me about discrimination and acceptance. I already knew about being "different." Now I learned what discrimination was.

By the time I entered third grade Myra had already been enrolled in and sent to Trenton State School for the Deaf [now the Marie F. Katzenback

School for the Deaf]. She lived there during the week and returned most weekends.

The predominantly Jewish neighborhood in which we lived was becoming older and deteriorating and Grandmother Esther thought it would be a good idea to consider moving to one of the suburbs, perhaps Union Township, where Max's brother, Philip, lived with his family. We could rely on him for help, too.

It was the Thursday before Good Friday 1956. All of us kids were excited about the prospect of Easter Vacation. Georgie and I made plans for what we were going to do during vacation and he decided to run home and get changed so we could play. I stayed in school a little longer to say goodbye to other friends. I finally left about 3:45PM. As I walked and turned the corner to our building there was a fire truck and an ambulance. Mrs. Samarin was waiting for me and immediately took me to her apartment. I was confused and asked why I couldn't go home. I'll never forget trying to look out her window with the attached fire escape. On the fire escape was the bottom of a roasting pan filled with dirt and the most beautiful pansies. I was mesmerized by the colors of the flowers. I wanted to see what was going on in the street and the reason for the big commotion. I had this strange feeling come over me. I wasn't sure what it was. I kept asking Mrs. Samarin what was wrong. Mrs. Samarin told me to wait until my mother picked me up and she would explain what happened.

Mother showed up at the Samarin apartment with the most horrific expression, almost as if it were the worst day of her life. She was white as a ghost and I could tell she had been crying. Always concerned for Mom's well-being I wanted to know what was wrong. "Georgie Krugman *dead*-hit by car" she told me. No. No. This couldn't be true! He had been running across the street separating our apartment building from his father's pharmacy. He briefly visited his father and was rushing home to change. Bolting out from between two cars, he was struck and killed. Although he didn't die immediately, he died with my Grandmother Esther beside him. She had rushed to be with him, holding his hand the whole time. I clearly remember the vision of his blood running down the cracks of the street and Grandmother Esther pouring kosher salt on it. The blood was also on her dress.

With Georgie's death, my childhood changed; I learned that death can and does change life in a split second.

Every time Georgie's mother saw me on the street she would become hysterical. My insides would tremble. I had no choice other than to avoid her…in silent pain.

CHAPTER NINE

MOVING TO THE SUBURBS...

Union Township, New Jersey is a small bedroom suburb of Newark. It is less than twenty miles from New York City. In 1956, many residents of the city of Newark moved to this then attractive community. It was dotted by older two story colonial bungalow type houses and cape cods built in the early 1900s.

My Uncle George had taken us for a ride to Union to look at properties.

On the street one block away from Dad's brother Philip's home there was a "For Sale" sign on an older colonial-style home. It sat on a small street with only four houses. It had a long driveway leading to a detached garage and a small back yard. Never having a yard in Newark, the yard looked like a farm to me.

George, Esther, Max and Nettie asked the owner the asking price. It was $15,500. My parents offered $15,000. The offer was immediately accepted. Generous Esther paid the five hundred dollar down payment. Off to the suburbs for us! It was considered an achievement when a deaf person bought a home. Mom and Dad were so pleased and proud.

We moved into our home August and everyone was so excited. We had three bedrooms, living room, dining room, kitchen, one (upstairs) bathroom, and even a basement in which to play. We were even going to have an automatic washing machine. Our lives appeared to be luxurious.

I was enrolled in Connecticut Farms Elementary school about a mile away. It was across the street from a beautiful old Presbyterian Church built around the time of the civil war. The church had a graveyard with very old gravestones we saw through the windows of the classroom. It made me uncomfortable. It seemed so mystical.

I unfortunately had to repeat the third grade due to some incongruous rule about cut-off dates and birthdates. I wasn't too happy about that but had no choice. Having already attended the third grade the previous year, I became the brainiac of Mrs. Tubin's third grade class. I guess I could say I was the teacher's pet. Many of my classmates teased me about this. I just plugged along doing my coursework. Being teased wasn't foreign to me; I had been teased since I could remember about my parents not being able to hear and speak. I was ridiculed for having "deaf and dumb" parents. Many of the kids would emphasize the '*dumb*' in the term "deaf and dumb." The dictionary definition of dumb is actually 'lacking the power of speech' but the kids didn't know that. My mother hated that term! To her it was derogatory. My father would say the hearing people that used that term were 'crazy'.

I desperately wanted to play the piano. Grandmother Esther purchased an old upright piano and said that if I practiced diligently that I would get a new one. I hated that old piano. It sounded tinny like an old ragtime piano. It could have been one hundred years old. I was precocious and could be devious so secretly I broke some of the hammers and the piano wouldn't play as it should. I begged for a new piano and my grandmother bought it for me. I was so happy and proud and became somewhat of a child prodigy. Music was an escape for me, it was a way to blur the real life challenges and responsibilities I faced. I took lessons until I was thirteen at which time I decided I had enough even though I had been offered the opportunity to play in the Catskill Mountain Resorts.

I made a few close friends in my neighborhood although I missed my best friend Georgie very much. There was Jim Swenson, a handsome blue-eyed blond Swedish boy. His parents had a very thick Swedish accent so he understood the meaning of being different.

As I grew I had an internal feeling of being different. I preferred girls as my friends because they were more sensitive and kind. The boys could be very cruel and often bullied me. I was more diminutive and sensitive than most of the boys and was an open target.

I knew my family was not like the other children's. My friends' parents were more protective, restrictive, and more involved with their children's education than my parents. My parents were busy just surviving.

I was emotionally mature as an adult at the age of eight. I could do almost anything I wanted. Today I am amazed that at that age my parents permitted me to take a bus from Union to downtown Newark by myself. Newark wasn't the safest city. They knew I would meet any challenge. There was a part of me that wanted them to say no. I would have felt more protected and loved. I had learned early in life how to survive, for the benefit of my family because it was my job. I always put my family first never realizing I wasn't fully developing a sense of my own self. My ego was fed by the good things I did for the family. That's just how it was, period.

Myra would come home for the weekends. She enjoyed being away at school and made many good friends. She was also dating a young man with whom she attended grade school. They had become sweethearts from the time they met.

I was ten when Myra became engaged. It was a very difficult time for the family because her fiancé was not Jewish. In those days marrying out of the religion was forbidden. In Orthodox Jewish law when a person married out of the religion the family was to sit Shiva, which is the ritual period of mourning after someone dies. The person was considered dead. There was much anger, fighting, crying and plain disappointment.

Grandmother Esther came to the rescue. Although she was quite religious she gathered the family to discuss the situation. She surprised the family when she said she would give their marriage her blessing. Her reasoning was these were two deaf people who first became friends then lovers. She couldn't understand why anyone would want to take away their joy. She told us that great love is not found everyday and the family *must* support her. The major source of conflict was the demand by the Catholic Church that the couple be married in the church and that Myra would sign a statement agreeing to raise future children as Catholic. She did not hesitate. My parents were adamant about not attending the church wedding. The acrimony seemed so silly to me. That was the beginning of my disassociation from organized religion. The day of the wedding, Grandmother Esther insisted we attend. Mother had said she wasn't going to buy a new dress for the wedding. But, the day of the wedding she took a box from the closet with a new dress. She had intended to go all along.

We were to accept this marriage unconditionally; that was the best choice. Grandmother Esther was truly a marvelous and compassionate woman. I admired her strength, her conviction, and adherence to the religion she so loved. I admired more her position that acts of love and love itself should be the ultimate goal in life and take precedence over all else.

Amongst much protest and conciliation, Myra was married in St Bridget's Catholic Church in Newark and whose priest was proficient in sign language. The marriage vows were repeated in sign. How I wished I had been encouraged to learn more of and become proficient in sign language. My mother actually discouraged it. Her desire for me not to learn more of sign language became detrimental and a major obstacle in my communication with the deaf.

With Myra leaving our household I became the only child at home. It wasn't strange since she was away at school anyway. The positive outcome for me was one less person for whom I was responsible. It may sound harsh but that is exactly the way I felt.

CHAPTER TEN

SWORN TO SILENCE...

Sex was a taboo subject in our home as it is in many. My mother was prudish about the subject and dad would coyly ignore any questions pertinent to it. I was told that babies come from swallowing a watermelon seed. Can you imagine how fearful I was when accidently I swallowed one? Most children my age, the age of ten, learned about the birds and the bees from either their parents or peers. I listened intently to what my friends were saying about it but really never perceived the whole concept. It seemed so foreign and weird. When a friend tried to explain the mechanics of it, it seemed disgusting. I absolutely couldn't imagine *my* parents doing *that!*

One day while at my cousin's home he went into his father's dresser drawer and pulled out a foil wrapper containing a condom. He opened it; we looked at it, and laughed. Exactly how it was used was beyond my comprehension. I feel it's so important for parents to educate their children about sex and love as early as the questions begin. Sex and love were two totally different concepts to me. So, when I was introduced to it I never equated the two could be perceived as one.

It was one fall day when it happened. My bedroom had twin beds, one for me and one for Myra that she used when she came home for the weekend and any guests that might visit. A deaf family friend was invited to stay overnight with us and given the spare bed in my room. I was asleep when I felt someone beside me. He was stroking me; touching my private parts. Although my parents had told me never to go with strangers they never explained that children should not allow adults to touch their genitals either. I experienced a whole range of feelings. But most of all I was frightened. It felt good physically but, emotionally I had so many thoughts going through my mind. Is this right? Did I have to do this? What is this anyway? What's happening to me? I was told never to tell anyone. I was to remain silent; this was 'our' secret. What painful silence it was to keep that secret.

The encounter lasted about an hour and resulted in my having my first orgasm. I was scared, horrified, and that hour changed my life forever. I had no idea what an ejaculation was and I had just had my first. My virginity was taken from me; taken too young. I was robbed of the opportunity to learn about sex on my own terms. Children must be taught their first experience should be of their own will and not under the control of another, especially an adult.

I thought something had gone wrong physically. What was wrong with me? This strange fluid had wet and stiffened my sheets. What would mother think when she would strip the sheets to wash them?

Since I was told never to tell anyone, never, I assumed I had done something wrong. I had no warning, no information that would have given me the knowledge and power to resist.

My life as a son, student, and friend changed, too. I had trouble making eye contact with my parents and other adults. I felt if an adult looked in my eyes they would know what I did. My grades started a slow slide downward. I wondered if my peers were doing the same thing. Any childhood happiness I might have had was replaced with confusion, fear, guilt, and shame. Life was just awful, a bundle of whirling emotions and confusion. I was unwillingly forced into sexual maturity. Between my strong familial responsibilities and being molested my life was plain hell.

Whenever this man was invited as a guest to our house he was given the extra bed in my room; I hated that bed. The molestation continued and my victimization of it as well. As it continued I learned about sex. I learned more than I ever wanted. Being a compliant child I became proficient at pleasing him. I also started to enjoy the perceived affection and attention towards me. I felt he loved me and in a way that was completely unfamiliar and not unwelcomed. Having these feelings is not unusual for victims of sexual abuse.

It's my guess that my friends had some inkling that I was becoming sexual. I would make sexual overtures and even had 'show and tell' sessions with some of my male peers. I knew way more than they and eventually they became reticent to continue our friendship. I was acting out. Losing the friendship of peers wasn't a big deal. I always related better to adults than children since I was far more mature, having to mature almost instantly taking on mountains of responsibility. Thankfully, nothing ever occurred with any other adult. Although the owner of the local candy store, an old shriveled up man made advances towards me. The thought of being with him made me sick. I ran out of the store and never went back! I wished my parents would have told me to tell them when things like this happened and to be more protective.

My emotions were always spinning like the whirlwind of a tornado. I had no one I could discuss my feelings with. My kindhearted father usually deferred dealing with his children's emotions to my mother who just didn't want to hear or deal with them. Later in life I realized that my parents had done the best with the knowledge they had.

I know that if my father knew what happened he would have killed the perpetrator – my dad's hobby was prizefighting! I could rarely approach mother with anything involving my emotions. She couldn't handle it. And, the way she responded to it was either saying 'forget it' or 'that's stupid'. She had learned this from her mother. Interestingly, as an adult when I finally told my mother about the molest she confessed that she, too, was molested by an uncle (her aunt's husband). Her way of coping was again to 'just forget' it. I learned to keep my experiences and feelings silent. There was no option. Burying noxious emotions and living in silence is a formula that almost always results in severe emotional pain.

I realize today that I was starved for attention and affection. I wanted to be loved for me and not the good deeds I performed. How many good deeds would it take for me to love *myself?*

At the age of thirteen I had what most Jewish boys entering adolescence have. I had a Bar-Mitzvah. The boy is called to the altar to read a portion of the Holy Torah. The boy's father reads from the Torah sometime during the service, too. Since my father was deaf, he sat silently on the altar in a place of honor and then silently stood next to me as I completed the reading. God, how I wished for my dad to hear!

My Bar-Mitzvah was held the Saturday after that of the son of the Rabbi, January 9, 1960. Boy, did I feel pressured to do well. I studied hard and I didn't miss a word. My voice was clear, in tune, and projected well. My voice was so good that after the ceremony, the Rabbi asked if I would consider training as a Cantor in the temple. I politely declined because it just wasn't my thing. I had had my fill of religious school and determined, at a young age with Myra's ordeal, that organized religion was not for me.

My grades in school continued to deteriorate. I became part of a clique that was called 'The Hoods' who wore leather jackets and were generally rebellious about everything including getting good grades. I tried to fit in but never felt truly accepted. I never fit in anywhere, neither with the n'er do wells or the college prep crowd. I wanted to be a part of any group; I wanted to belong. I just didn't know where I fit; I was in a world of my own in silence.

Peer acceptance is very important in the development of a child's self-esteem and confidence. My self-perception, esteem and confidence were built mostly by my good deeds and helping to resolve family issues.

It was only through these acts that I knew I was doing something worthwhile. The "family guest" visits continued as well as the physicality through mid adolescence. I was about sixteen when I finally realized I didn't have to comply. I finally came to realize I had the right to control my own activities; and being with him was not one of them. I ended it. That decision started me on the long road to recovery and empowerment. I never allowed myself to be alone in the same room or circumstances that might be to his advantage. I thought, finally, I might have peace.

Any survivor of incest or molestation will tell you that peace and resolution of the victimization of incest or molestation doesn't come easy. The feelings of anger, fear, guilt, and shame stick to the emotional part of the brain like glue.

It was only with professional help as an adult that the emotions associated with the molestation were resolved. I hoped someday I would survive the pain initiated by the silence of both deafness and molestation. Progressing through the process from victim to survivor was emotionally painful and it took years of therapy to unravel the emotional damage.

Being a victim, I felt subordinate, like my parents, 'less than' others; as a survivor I'm triumphant.

As a teenager my mother would take me to downtown Newark on Saturdays when she had her hair done. I intensively watched as Gabriel, her hairdresser, beautified her coif. I remember being fascinated by his techniques such as coloring and teasing which was popular in those days. I developed an interest in this line of work I asked my parents to allow me to enroll in the Wilfred Beauty Academy in Newark. They preferred that I go to college like all my cousins. My mother used my cousins as an example of whom I should emulate. "Why can't you be like your cousins?" I was relentless in my desire and they reluctantly gave me permission.

I attended both high school and Wilfred at the same time. My classes at Wilfred were two nights a week and Saturdays. My strong passion for my studies as an up and coming stylist gave me something to feel great about. I was becoming one of the best students in the school. I had no focus on my high school grades. I just didn't care about them and they further deteriorated.

Eventually the chemical odors and sprays exacerbated my asthmatic condition and I was forced to drop out. Leaving this career path wasn't all that sad because I had come to realize that a male interested in becoming a hair stylist was often labeled 'queer' or 'homo' or other derogatory names. I suffered in silence often when I was taunted with these names. I had been called enough names during

my childhood. I dreamed of being just like every other
'normal' boy.

The Franklin (Futoronsky) Family – Fanny & Joseph with Children

Morris (Wisokofsky) Weiss – Grandfather Standing (with his hat) in the factory

Esther Franklin Weiss – Grandmother Age 19

Mom & Dad (Nettie & Max)
Wedding date: January 3, 1936

Dad prior to his marriage…

Dad at his Newsstand!

I was three years of age and loved this pony!
Mom, Dad & I
I, at twelve months.

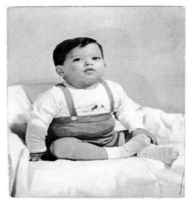

Myra & Me…Myra was never happy at having a brother; she wanted a sister!

Mom (she was so pretty), Me, at the old upright piano I hated, and Dad, Mom, Grandma Esther and I.

Myra, my daughter Gayle, mom and I - Mom's last week prior to her passing.

CHAPTER ELEVEN

SURVIVING MOLESTATION AND VICTIMIZATION

The basic definition of survivor is one who remains alive and who can carry on life despite hardships or trauma. But, to me, surviving is more than just the ability to carry on life. It is the ability to work through the emotional issues that can prevent us from being the self-actualized person we want to be. It isn't enough to just exist; life is about being the best we can be with what we are given.

Loss of self esteem, anger, depression, guilt, shame, feelings of inferiority, feelings of not 'fitting in' are common amongst survivors of sexual abuse. My anger was directed at my parents for not protecting me. But they were busy with their own challenges and just didn't know better. For that, they're forgiven.

To hold on to the negative emotions that are a result of the abuse is to allow the perpetrator to continue to hold power over us. I didn't know how to resolve those issues until I sought counseling. I learned that the abuse was a method of power; an adult having power over a child – something that is absolutely unacceptable.

For years I was so ashamed and guilty about what I allowed to transpire. It felt both good and bad. The physical pleasure was the basic expression of the human body. The emotional connection was addictive. I thought I was loved; it was exciting and rewarding that my perpetrator remained attracted to me.

Until I had entered therapy I didn't understand that I was starved for attention and love. The desire to be loved can be addictive and can result in poor choices if not consciously understood. As a child I was able to make mature choices and communicate on a mature level. But beneath my unusually adult abilities I was just a child yearning for connection and attention without all the layers I developed since I was very young.

Recovering from abuse is empowering. Empowerment results from the ability to analyze, evaluate, understand, and resolve the feelings that one is not in control. Counseling is what helped me. I've come far in the long and hard road of recovery. I now never allow anyone to even think they have control over me. My boundaries are set and when they are crossed I act immediately.

I was a victim and my life felt that way until I had no choice other to change. It would have been emotional death had I let the feelings of victimization continue. Recognizing victimization is a primary step in taking control of one's life. Shoving the abuse under the carpet is seriously debilitating. The emotions arising from the abuse will find there way out in acts and feelings that can be undesirable.

I'm not ashamed to share my abuse with other men. To my chagrin I have found many have experienced it also. My goal was not to just cope with the effects, it was to rise above them, stand on the mountain and reach the epitome of self-actualization. Ironically, I became who I am because of the energy and persistence to climb that mountain.

CHAPTER TWELVE
YOU'LL NEVER BE ANYTHING!

Surviving is just about what I did most of the time. My grades were poor; just above passing. My social life both in high school and at home was poor also. Although I had a few close friends, I felt so different from them. I had one girl friend, Jackie, with whom I did just about everything. We would skip school, drink, party, and generally goof off. I liked the buzz I got from drinking. It seemed to cushion my emotions. Little did I realize at that time that I was an addict. My drug of choice was the need for approval and attention that came from my role as family advocate. I liked when people I knew or didn't know thought that I was the most incredible person for assuming the responsibilities I did.

I wasn't an average teenager. Whenever I had the chance I partied and drank in excess. I also drove drunk. When I look back at those days I realize I was using the alcohol to cover the many emotions that were always with me. I remember one particular time I was driving [while drunk] hitting a divider and the car flying over it. I'm amazed I made it without a scratch! I was sure there was divine intervention.

Fortunately, my IQ was high enough that although my grades were poor, I never really studied. Neither my career path nor life path had any focus.

I was living one day at a time meeting the challenges that seemed to come from every direction.

In high school we had regular visits with our guidance counselors. The counselor assigned to me was Mrs. Charlotte Dane, a tall thin woman with shiny black hair slicked back in a bun. She always reminded me of "Olive Oil" the cartoon figure in the television series 'Popeye the Sailor Man.'

Her demeanor was cold and abrasive and I found no comfort when she told me that I would never achieve anything in life. I wasn't sure if she made that statement for shock value or if she really meant it. Whatever the case may be her opinion woke me up. I was so angry she made that statement and without a doubt I intended to prove her wrong. When I fixed my mind on something I was unstoppable!

I was a senior in high school when Mrs. Dane made that fateful and profound statement. My grades were disappointing low Cs and my curriculum was general education, not college prep. I decided I wanted to be like the other students, to go to college, to have a career, and my own family someday. I longed to have my own 'normal' family. "Normal" was something I was consistently trying to achieve. If only I had understood earlier that 'normal' doesn't necessarily represent [the beauty of] uniqueness.

No college would accept me as an applicant because I didn't take the college prep curriculum. Mrs. Dane told me I could enroll in Newark Preparatory School for one year and take the necessary courses and college boards to increase my chances of a college acceptance. I did just that.

My grades in prep school were straight As. I especially excelled in Spanish and 'Mr. G' [most people had difficulty in pronouncing his last name] my Spanish Professor encouraged me to become a Spanish teacher. My proficiency in languages became quite evident and I accepted his recommendation and decided in college I would major in Spanish.

As a senior in prep school I applied to and was accepted to Edward Williams College, a junior college affiliated with Fairleigh Dickinson University located in Teaneck, NJ. I continued to be an excellent and dedicated student. As usual, I did very well in my Spanish classes and also developed an affinity for my elective courses in Psychology.

I took many Psychology courses and aced them. Like other students majoring in Psychology it was interesting because I thought I could learn more about myself and heal my own wounds. I frequently made Dean's list, too. I was in a bakery one afternoon when Mrs. Dane walked in. I gloated when she asked me how I was doing. "I'm pleased to tell you, Mrs. Dane, that I've made Dean's List. Her reaction was a smirk. I would have welcomed more of a positive response but, oh well, I vindicated myself.

If only she had recognized the signs of abuse perhaps I could have been helped through the silent pain that plagued me. Today, Guidance Counselors are trained to look for signs of abuse and help students through recovery process. Today there are many effective avenues to help victims of abuse; it has unfortunately become so common. Statistically, one in six boys in the United States is sexually abused.

As I mentioned, I became a good student focusing on achieving my degree. But, behind my focus emotional pain still permeated the creases of my brain.

CHAPTER THIRTEEN

I WANT A NORMAL FAMILY

During my college days I didn't date much. I was focused on achieving good grades and graduating college as early as possible. I wanted to make up the time lost by having to attend Prep School. I wanted to go away to college, to live in the dorms and experience the freedom a young man should. But, I felt guilty about leaving my parents and decided commuting to college would be the best decision. Decisions about *my* life were secondary. I was not as important as they. Gratefully, I managed to graduate in three and a half years.

Prior to my last semester in college [August 1968], my friend, Jerry, arranged a blind date for me. My friend gave me one caveat which was this girl really wanted to get married. That didn't bother me in the least because I did, too. Marsha and I hit it off immediately. We dated for six weeks prior to becoming engaged. I was thrilled and on my way to starting my own family.

Although my parents supported my decision and helped pay for the engagement ring I knew that Mom had an undercurrent of sadness at my leaving the home. I couldn't wait for my freedom. Dad, as usual, was fine with my decision. As for my grandmother, Esther, I knew her concern was that I was not going to be as available for the very responsibilities she taught me to assume. I would never have thought to relinquish *any* responsibility for my deaf family. I knew what was expected and always followed through.

Marsha and I were married August 31, 1969 in a beautiful Jewish Ceremony and honeymooned in New York's Catskill Mountains. One of the places we stayed was Motel in the Mountain which eventually and ironically was converted to a gay resort.

After the long honeymoon weekend we returned to our apartment in Highland Park, NJ. Marsha continued her career as a bi-lingual (English-Spanish) secretary and I continued my last semester of studies towards my Bachelor's Degree.

Six weeks after we married Marsha became ill with what appeared to be an intestinal problem. She was nauseous, fatigued, and we were generally concerned about her health. After a trip to the doctor we were given the news that she was pregnant! She had become pregnant on our honeymoon! I was out of my mind with joy. She was not. She was frightened that it was too soon, and that our lives would change forever. She had rarely been exposed to babies and didn't know how to feed, diaper, and care for one. However, it didn't take much time for her to be accustomed to the idea of becoming a mother. She enjoyed being pregnant saying that she always had 'company'.

May 28, 1970 I returned late in the evening after taking a civil service test for a job as a Social Worker. Marsha was six days overdue. We went to bed and at two o'clock am she woke me saying she was having contractions. I asked her if the contractions were inconsistent or regular. She said inconsistent coming about every 5 to 7 minutes. Since I was an "expert" in labor in childbirth after taking a six week course in LaMaze [natural childbirth] I told her it was false labor and to go back to sleep. I fell asleep and awoke at seven in the morning with Marsha pacing back and forth. She said the pain was more intense but still irregular like every two and four minutes. Still thinking this was false labor I didn't take her seriously until she insisted I take some action. I called the obstetric department of St. Peter's Hospital in New Brunswick, NJ and asked to speak with an obstetric nurse. After discussing Marsha's condition she said I had better bring her in immediately. This was NOT false labor…it was the REAL thing! It took us about a half an hour to arrive at the hospital. An hour and a half later at 9:30 AM on May 29, 1970 our dear daughter Gayle Ilene was born. She fulfilled the dream of having my own family. I was now the Patriarch of my own 'normal' family. Gayle was not deaf. I didn't know until after she was born that Marsha had terrible fear that our child might be deaf. She later told me that if we were going to have more children she wanted genetic counseling.

Gayle was born two days prior to my college graduation which I didn't attend. Caring for Marsha and Gayle was more important than receiving my degree in person. I had also just secured a position as Bi-Lingual Social Worker (Spanish-English) with a local government agency and wanted to prepare for my start date.

Marsha left her job as a Bi-Lingual Secretary to become a full-time mother. Gayle was a pink bundle of joy and Marsha didn't want to drop her off in child care as many of the young mothers were doing. She felt parenthood was a full-time responsibility and took to it well.

CHAPTER FOURTEEN

LOSING DAD

Dad and I had never been very close. Mom and Dad's relationship was one of sheer tolerance and convenience. I had known for many years theirs was a loveless marriage. Perhaps any respect Mom had for Dad was dimmed by the fact that he always carried the picture of his former fiancé in his wallet. Perhaps she really never loved him and married because two could meet the challenges of their silent world better than one. The blatant evidence was just there, I could feel it…it was a loveless marriage. Dad just went about the business of working and watching baseball games on TV (NY Mets was his favorite team). In the summer he would sit in front of the TV with a handkerchief wrapped around his neck to keep him cool. Mom would complain about almost everything he did and I was her sounding board. She was convincing about her marital unhappiness and I unconditionally sided with her.

Becoming a father made me more aware of what my dad experienced in being a parent himself. As Gayle grew from infancy to toddlerhood I developed increasing respect and admiration for him.

I had always liked the autumn in NJ with the leaves turning beautiful shades of orange, red, yellow, and purple. It was a beautiful day when Marsha, Gayle, and I went shopping in one of the local malls. I was pushing Gayle in the stroller and Marsha was looking at clothes. We always enjoyed shopping together as a family.

We arrived home about one thirty in the afternoon on Saturday October 2, 1971 and sat down to have lunch. The phone rang and it was my father's brother, my uncle Al. Al never had much contact with us so I was surprised to hear from him. His voice was sad and he said I needed to come immediately to my parents' home. "Why" I asked? He said "Ben, your dad is very sick." I answered that my dad was as healthy as a horse and was *never* sick. I could hear the tension in his voice. I knew he was holding something back. Then I asked him to tell me the truth. When he did I dropped the phone and just stood and stared into space. He told me Dad had not felt well the previous day. He had a backache and went to the doctor who performed many tests including an EKG. The doctor said the ache was due to muscle spasms and prescribed a muscle relaxant. Dad had gone to sleep early that night. The next morning Mom thought Dad was sleeping unusually long. She felt he needed to rest and gave him until eleven o'clock am to wake. When he didn't awaken by that time she went up and tried to wake him. There was no movement and he was cold. He had died; he passed away in his sleep.

We immediately drove to the home where I grew up. In addition to my dad's brothers and sister-in-laws, Myra was there. She had an intuition that something was wrong. She lived half a mile away and decided to check. Driving to the house she saw the ambulance and the hearse, and immediately knew she had lost her dad. My sister, mother, and I were very intuitive. She and Dad were very close; he was her mentor in deafness, in sign language, in navigating the world of silence. Her hero was gone on this beautiful fall day. Fall was never the same for me – it always reminds me of death. I'm glad I live in California now!

As customary in the Jewish religion, Dad's funeral was the next day. On Sunday, October 3, 1971 Dad was laid to rest. Beth Israel Cemetery in Woodbridge, NJ is a beautiful park-like setting. Sitting in front of the casket as it was lowered a strong breeze blew my Yarmulke from my head onto the top of his casket as it was lowered. Everyone gasped – the symbolism behind this was so strong. A piece of me went with him. My Aunt Florence whispered in my ear "Benson – I can't believe what just happened"!

Shiva is the customary Jewish tradition regarding the initial period of mourning after someone dies. It usually lasts seven days. We were comforted by many friends and relatives bringing great meals and sweets. One day during Shiva while Myra and I were sitting on the front porch Mom came out with Dad's black onyx pinky ring. She handed it to me and said that my dad would have wanted me to have it. I placed it on my finger. Suddenly, I felt this tremendous slap and pain across my face. Myra was enraged that I had been given this heirloom. I, at first, couldn't comprehend what just happened. I thought perhaps it was her jealousy at my being 'hearing.' Or she may have wanted the ring for herself. She always complained that I was the 'privileged child' and received more than she. Truthfully, if I were favored, I deserved it. I earned it living through the years of caretaking and losing my childhood. Years later I gave Myra the ring hoping our relationship would improve. Although we loved each other there were no common interests and she was much older. Our kinship as mature brother and sister never fully blossomed. When I asked her if she envied that I could hear her answer was 'absolutely not' and that she was proud of who she is. We are two different people in two different worlds. There is deafening silence between us to this day.

The healing of the relationship that was developing between Dad and me was cut short. I always hoped and will hope that he understood how much I loved and respected him.

Mom and Grandmother Esther were now alone. I continued to assume responsibilities relating Mom's and now my aging grandmother's health and general well-being in addition to my own as a husband and father. To say responsibility was my middle name would have been to make the understatement of the century. I now had more responsibility then ever.

As a mature adult I always sought to improve myself. I enrolled in Rider's College Master's in Public Administration Degree Program. The extra commute, class work, and exams created increasing stress.

But, I was determined; I was going to make sure Mrs. Dane's prediction was wrong. I wanted to be *someone*.

Just who that someone was I really didn't know. As I struggled and strove for more and more success in both my career and schoolwork, Marsha and I started to grow apart. It was my nature and desires to express my emotions and communicate my fears and share my feelings with those close to me. Marsha tended to be more introspective and preferred to keep things to herself. But I sure knew when she was angry or upset. Her desire not to share just exacerbated how much I hated silence.

CHAPTER FIFTEEN

THE MATRIARCH PASSES

Although Dad's passing was a shock and made me sad I handled the grief well. I didn't feel as responsible for him as I did my mother and sister. Dad was quite independent and, as I've said, content with being deaf. He was just a happy guy. My sadness arose from feeling that we never had the opportunity to connect on a father to son level. I thought my mother's unhappiness was caused by Dad and I lost respect for him. Only in death did I realize the true impact of his love and values on me. I wish I could have him in front of me for one minute. He'd know how much love I had for him.

Mother had learned to drive and absolutely loved it. It gave her a sense of freedom. She even got a job to which she had to commute about forty five minutes each way. She didn't mind. Driving was an escape for her. She was in her own world when she was driving in her car. Even two weeks prior to her death when she was paralyzed from the waist down she insisted a physical therapist come to help her walk so she could drive.

Subsequent to Dad's death it was Mom and Grandmother Esther alone in the family home in Union. Their daily routine consisted of Mom driving Grandmother to the store to buy fresh meat and vegetables. Grandmother pronounced it "weg-a-tbls" in her Russian accent. Although I was glad that Mom had her mother living with her I never stopped my vigilance for their well-being.

Grandmother always made sure I knew she wasn't going to live forever. She would always say "Benson, when I die I want your mother to live with you." "I'm not going to live forever". She would tell me that she had lived long enough and that it was 'time.' She was just plain tired of living. I was distressed when she said this. I loved her like a mother. She and I, as her protégé caretaker, were partners in assuring Mom stayed content and well. The responsibility for my family was drilled into my psyche by her since the moment I understood the English language.

Our family home had two flights of stairs, one leading to the second floor with the three bedrooms and one leading to the basement where the washer and dryer were located. Grandmother was becoming increasingly frail and the stairs were a burden. It was then I insisted that Mom sell the house and buy a condo nearby my home. Mom loved the idea; grandmother didn't. She wanted to remain in the house that was so familiar to her, where she had seen her granddaughter married and her son-in-law die. She wanted to sit on the porch and reminisce about her past, her joys, and sorrows and live her remaining days. She wanted to die in that home.

I pursued the issue of moving and made it clear to Mom and Grandmother the decision I made for them to move was in their best interest. I arranged for a real estate agent to list the home. The "For Sale" sign went up in front of the house on a Sunday. The next day the agent showed the house to prospective buyers who entered into a contract to purchase the home. While the agent was there, Grandmother fell on the stairs leading to the second floor. The agent called me and said she had taken her to the doctor. The doctor said Grandmother was frail but there was no need to take her to the hospital. My concern was growing deeper and I wanted them near me *soon*.

The following Wednesday at about five thirty in the afternoon I had just returned from work when a neighbor of Mom's called me to tell me that Grandmother had been rushed to the hospital. She had collapsed in the bathroom. Mom had run to the neighbor's home to ask her to call me. I immediately drove to Mom's home and we drove to the hospital. Grandmother was on a stretcher in the emergency room and complaining of abdominal pain.

The doctor's were going to run tests to determine the cause. She begged me for 7UP. She was very thirsty. The doctor would not permit her to have either liquids or solids. She kept asking for a drink and it broke my heart not to comply with her request. After consultation with her regular physician who came to the hospital to examine her, the final diagnosis was that my grandmother had hardening of the arteries. She was having small strokes and cardiac issues and she would not be able to go home. Her mental and physical condition was severely compromised. She would need to be placed in a nursing home. This couldn't be happening to my grandmother; the woman I knew who had tremendous strength and courage. I told Mom what the doctor said and we both sat dazed looking at the sterile walls of the hospital.

We left the hospital and since I didn't want Mom to be alone I drove Mom to my house for the night. I silently prayed that Grandmother would pass if she had to be institutionalized. It would devastate all of us. At midnight the phone rang. I knew immediately it was not good news. No one would call that late unless there was an emergency. It was the nurse in the intensive care unit in the hospital informing me that Grandmother had taken a turn for the worse and to get to the hospital as soon as we could. We picked up Myra and arrived at the hospital about two in the morning. When we arrived in the intensive unit the nurse said she was failing quickly. We went to her bedside where she lay with an oxygen mask. Her eyes had a blank stare. She was in a coma. The three of us sat in the hallway – we couldn't bear to watch her. As her condition worsened and death was approaching, the nurse asked if we wanted to be with her as she passed. I was a mature man of twenty six yet I shuddered at the thought of watching her die. I didn't want her to die; I just couldn't do it and declined. The three of us decided to remain outside the room in the hallway. It was then I heard the famous 'code blue.' I knew the old Russian peasant woman I so adored had passed.

The sound of the gurney removing her body rattled through my head.

We left the hospital about three thirty in the morning and headed for our family home in Union, the home with so many memories. When Grandmother was alive I always heard the clunking of her Wide Side Kid shoes on the bare steps. She had a strong and determined stride. Walking into the house after her passing I heard those same footsteps. I swear it was Grandmother! It was truly eerie. Mom refused to ever step in the house again.

I grieved not only the loss of her presence, but her old country mannerisms, and her love of family. Family always came first to her. She had a Strong and protective attitude. I also grieved the loss of any freedom I might have from the responsibilities she told me I must assume upon her passing. I had my own family challenges, my studies and now total responsibility for my mother. I felt torn in a hundred different pieces and directions.

Grandmother died on Thursday, March 8, 1973. The next day, Friday, was her funeral. Mom, Myra and I sat in the back of the limousine that took us from the funeral home to the cemetery. I was terribly grief stricken and numb. I don't remember much about the funeral except sobbing 'Ma!' as her plain pine casket was lowered into the grave. For me, grief is one of the most painful of human emotions. It feels like a serrated knife cutting through the heart. Only with time does the wound heal.

I scrapped the idea of moving Mom into a condo [the family house had sold]. Instead I found her a cute apartment close to my family and me. Mom wasn't thrilled with the idea of living alone. She consistently reminded me that Grandmother always said she should live with me after Grandmother's passing. I felt my family and I needed our own space and to live as a 'normal' family. I was always seeking what I perceived as 'normal'. A few years later when Mom and I had a disagreement about an issue, she said she could *never* live with me – what a relief!

My personal and career pressures were exacerbated by the grief and guilt that was building since Grandmother's death. Guilt, why should I feel guilty? I felt guilty that I wasn't giving my mother as much attention as she wanted. I knew that my wife wasn't exactly thrilled with my mother needing so much attention, too.

It was only five days after my grandmother passed when I received a call at my office that my dad's brother, Sol, had died suddenly. I attended his funeral exactly one week after that of my grandmother's. His grave was within a short distance from that of my grandmother's. Looking at my grandmother's newly dug grave was unbearable.

Five weeks after my uncle's death Marsha's dad died suddenly. She was devastated. She closed herself in our bedroom for a week. She was silent, morose, and grief-stricken. I wanted her to share her feelings with me but she just couldn't. We had so many deaths in that short period of time that I actually

106

became afraid to answer the telephone. It seemed as though death was hovering over my head. I felt as though there were a curse on our family. How could I not answer the phone; the very vehicle that became so much a part of me? The telephone and I were one. I felt alone in a silence which I couldn't penetrate. My life was freefalling.

CHAPTER SIXTEEN

THE BREAKING POINT

I thought I was a strong man capable of meeting most any challenge and holding things together whether personally or in my career. I graduated with an undergraduate degree in Psychology and was sure I could analyze, evaluate, and fix anything and anybody. I could never have been so wrong.

After I secured a great job with the Middlesex County Board of Social Services as a Social Worker I was climbing the corporate ladder and was rapidly promoted to manager. I was honored, too, when I was appointed a Union Negotiator for local 1082 of the Communications Workers of America. I was proud of my accomplishments and proud of my family.

I had a family and career but still had the lingering grief over the loss of my Grandmother. And I had a mother for whom I was one hundred per cent responsible.

Yes, I was on the paved road to success. Just look at me world, I was a success! I desperately wanted attention focused on me that wasn't related to caring for the deaf. I wanted to be recognized for my individual persona, period.

Chronic fatigue became part of me; I lived with it all my waking hours. I was eating more to alleviate my stress and gaining pounds by the day. Life felt as though it were one vicious circle. The circle included work, going to college at night, helping Marsha around the house, helping with our child's needs, and caring for Mom. Mom was *never* left out of the picture.

Studying for my Master's Degree, my classes were every Tuesday and Thursday from 7PM to 10PM and the campus was one hour from where we lived. It was a Thursday when I left work and headed to the Trenton Campus of Rider College which was about an hour from where we lived. The traffic was horrendous on Route 18 - bumper to bumper, horns honking, and drivers angrily flailing their hands and flipping each other off. It was just plain miserable. I became more fearful that I wouldn't make it to class. Then it happened.

Sitting in the driver's seat I started to shake, sweat, cry, and my heart was palpitating so that I thought I was going to die. I had never felt so awful, it was a feeling I never want to experience again. I didn't think I was going to be able to turn around and go home. I panicked and my heart was beating a thousand times a minutes. Suffering, I slowly, miraculously, and painstakingly returned home. When I arrived home Marsha knew something was wrong. I was white as a ghost. The shaking didn't stop and Marsha tried to comfort me. I felt as though I were in another world. I felt alone in the anguish of this emotional and physical hell that surrounded me. My symptoms worsened and I felt as though I was enveloped by darkness, a black cloud filled with anxiety, shame, grief, guilt, anger, and sadness of unbelievable proportion.

Arising the next morning I felt no different. I had no choice though but then to get out of bed and drag myself to work. I felt as if all the blood had been drained from my face. The corners of my mouth would not cooperate in creating a smile and I felt just like a walking corpse.

Since my education was in Psychology I knew that this was a panic attack. But it was one round-the-clock continuous feeling of panic wrapped around all the other emotions I had at the time. Perhaps I could help myself, perhaps I could recover quickly, and perhaps I wouldn't have to seek professional help. Perhaps I was wrong. I was dead wrong.

The physical symptoms were becoming unbearable. I was shivering cold most of the time, losing my hair, and gaining weight at an astronomical pace. Marsha forced me to seek medical help and I did. For one year I went from doctor to doctor begging for help and each time I was told it was my 'nerves' and given a sedative. One doctor gave me a sedative so powerful that I collapsed.

How I ever maintained my career and any semblance of sanity is only by the grace of God. I temporarily gave up my goal of achieving my Master's Degree. My immediate goal was to regain my strength.

I didn't share my anguish with my mother. Her inability to understand and deal with my emotions along with her stoic nature made it difficult for me to share mine with her.

I was referred to an Internal Medicine Specialist and sat in his examination room anxiously waiting for him. I was sure I was going to be told this was just another case of these symptoms 'being in my head.' He walked in asked me a few questions, looked at my scalp, my skin, and listened to my heart. He said he was sure I had Hashimoto's Thyroidism (underactive thyroid) and ordered blood tests which came back positive one week later. He told me that it was not unusual for this condition to be provoked by stress. I started on thyroid replacement hormone and slowly improved but never to the point where I had no physical and/or emotional symptoms. I was twenty seven years of age and feeling very fragile.

I decided to seek psychological help, too. The first psychiatrist I consulted turned out to be a nut of unbelievable proportions. All he did was talk about his wife and how a man should be the 'cock of the walk' in his own home. A year Later, I discovered he and his wife (also a psychiatrist) divorced. I decided to help myself become stronger emotionally and read every self-help book I could find. I was able to maintain a semblance of stability but always never felt I fully regained my strength.

During this time our marriage faltered more. I had become very difficult to live with. I would blow up at the drop of a hat. I also found it difficult and frustrating that my wife couldn't share her feelings with me. Silence was never a friend or peace to me. I later learned that Marsha was dealing with her own demons.

It was August of 1974 when Marsha had a cold and missed menstruating. She thought it was due to her cold and called her Gynecologist who gave her pills to hasten its arrival. He also said if she did not start within seven days she should come in for a pregnancy test. The cold left but neither did the menstruation arrive. She was pregnant. We both had a difficult time with this discovery. We knew our marriage was troubled and I was still not well. After speaking with a number of friends and relatives we decided the pregnancy, although a surprise could bring positive results.

Bryan Robert Garfinkle was born April 2, 1975 weighing 8lbs 3 oz. He was a big bruiser. When I heard his first cry I knew that he was going to be more than a handful. Marsha had fallen on the ice when she was seven months pregnant. In utero he turned feet first, a breech, and was born by cesarean section.

After his birth I felt well enough to think about returning to my desire to achieve my advanced degree. In spite of my illness I was dedicated to my career and was promoted to Personnel Director. I changed my educational direction to focus on a degree in Human Resources and Industrial Relations. Rutgers University, nearby our home had the curriculum I sought. I enrolled and took my first three courses at night and aced them.

My life seemed fairly stable at this point but then I hit another bump in the road. Due to strict civil service regulations and circumstances beyond my control I was forced to leave the job I loved and was promoted, under protest, to a higher level of management administering welfare programs. I had been involved with the administration of these programs earlier in my career and didn't want this type of work or the promotion.

I had no choice; the promotion was mandatory. Also, the manager to whom I was going to report had a reputation of being very difficult. The passion for my career, my life and health was spiraling downward once again.

After much discussion with Marsha, I left my government position and went to work as a Corporate Recruiter. I was so successful that within six months I opened my own Recruitment Firm. With the demands of the business my stress ballooned.

The panic attacks, the anger, the guilt, shame and depression that attacked me years back were with me again. My hostility towards Marsha, myself, and anyone who had contributed to making my life difficult was unbearable. I was so fatigued I couldn't get out of bed. The black cloud of depression once again had surrounded me. I know I was just a bear to live with and being a bear was and is not my true nature. Something was wrong and I needed help. Not only were my emotions out of control but so was my body. I felt as if my mind and body were falling apart piece by piece.

Because of my symptoms nutrition became my interest and I hoped that through good nutrition I would improve. While in a local health food store one day I met a woman with whom I started a conversation about my symptoms.

Hers were similar, too. She was recovering from her illness and I was keenly interested in what she was doing. She recommended I be seen by the physicians at a progressive facility called (at the time) Princeton Brain Bio Center, headed by noted physician Dr. Carl Pfeiffer.

I was seen by Dr. Camo who seemed to be very knowledgeable about people with symptoms such as mine. As a matter of fact, she told me she also had these symptoms years past and was now fine.

There were many questions, many tests, and I returned a few weeks after the completion of the tests for the results. I was confused, scared, and then relieved when Dr. Camo gave me the results. I finally had a diagnosis. My illness was not in my head! I was diagnosed with a rare hematological condition called Pyroluria which is a hybrid of a rare form of Porphyria. The illness is caused by a defect in the production of hemoglobin and very much related to the adrenal glands. When the adrenal glands are stressed due to anger, grief, etc., it triggers the hemoglobin to manufacture what is called a pyrolle. These pyrolles bind to the vitamins and minerals in the blood, specifically Zinc, Manganese and Vitamin b-6 and excrete abnormal amounts through the urine.

The result of this is that the body becomes nutritionally deficient causing fatigue, depression, obsessions, and sometimes delusions. There is no cure for this condition except the supplementation of the lost minerals and vitamins. Pyroluria tends to be a familial-hereditary defect that can be seen in almost ten percent of individuals with chronic fatigue and emotional/mental challenges. There is a test for it in the US but the condition is not recognized in this country as a traditional diagnosis since it can't be cured by medicine. In Europe this test is given quite routinely and the diagnosis is well-recognized and accepted.

I was cautioned to keep my stress under control (quite a feat), eat nutritiously, cut out sugar and carbohydrates, rest, and eat basically nutritious and whole foods. I recovered slowly from the debilitating affects of this illness and have been thankful that I was never hospitalized. I am eternally grateful to Dr. Pfeiffer and the Princeton Brain Bio Center for their work in the realm of this illness.

I always plugged away to achieve my career goals, even in my most sick moments. During this time my business was booming and most of my clients were in California. After having made numerous business trips to beautiful California I decided it would be best for the family to relocate there. We packed up our two children, three dogs and settled in a beautiful community in Orange County, California.

I felt the move was a good idea not only for business but for the relationship between Mother and me. I wanted distance between us. I wanted her to be more independent. I wanted to demonstrate to Marsha that I could weaken the ties between my mother and myself. Little did I know the emotional ties to her could not be severed by distance. I *never* stopped worrying about her.

I'll never forget her facial expression when she visited us the day of our big move. The moving truck was pulling away and we were readying ourselves to leave for the airport. The expression on Mom's face was one of grief and sorrow. I could barely look at her. Deep in my soul I knew I couldn't let the separation from her last too long. I suffered from such tremendous guilt. It was then I realized I, in an unhealthy way, was dependent upon her needs. Her dependency on me was my ego's addiction. The concern, worry, and pain were uncontrollable.

CHAPTER SEVENTEEN
CRAVING NORMALCY

There was never a day that I didn't crave a normal life including a wife, children, and to just blend into the average population. I wasn't average though. I was a driven man seeking self-fulfillment through material things. My ego needed to be fed. My personality wasn't average either. I'm a charismatic individual to whom people are drawn and open their souls (training to be a psychotherapist helps). I can remember a specific time when I worked for the Board of Social Services. I had one hundred fifty people reporting to me. One of my subordinates asked if she could speak with me. Answering, 'yes' I asked what she'd like to discuss. She didn't want to discuss anything. She wanted to tell me she thought I was one of the most charismatic people she'd ever met. Can you believe I wanted to crawl under my desk when I heard that comment? I wanted to be just like everyone else; I didn't want to be different and with her observation I felt it. I was always *different*.

Deep inside the bowels of my soul I was unhappy. I was always looking for projects to divert my mind away from my real issues. I felt as if I were acting; that life was just one big stage and I was the headline with no audience. There were thoughts of suicide, too. But how could I do *that*...I had so many people depending on me.

For all intensive purposes, people perceived me and my family as a loving, cohesive, and successful unit. But, the chatter in my mind never stopped. I wanted more and more. I realize now that when people are unhappy they find projects to occupy their minds. "Projects" may include *other* love interests, too.

I'm proud of the fact that during our twenty three year marriage I was faithful even though I had many opportunities to negate that. I have always felt that monogamy is included in calculating one's integrity.

I had a pervasive nagging in my mind and soul as to whom I really was. I was confused. I knew I was attracted to the same sex yet knew that many men and women are, also. That didn't mean they were gay. To me, they were gay if they acted upon their desires. The nagging in my mind continued and I decided to seek professional help to sort out my feelings. Oh, how I wanted to be normal! I had a wonderful psychiatrist who, after many sessions, convinced me that I was not gay, just somewhat confused and that my feelings were within the 'normal' range. For some time I accepted his assessment. As more time passed I realized his evaluation was just plain wrong. I *was* different.

Marsha and I were moving in different directions and our relationship was increasingly more. We were married for twenty three years when we mutually decided to end the partnership. I was sad and fearful about being alone for the first time. My dream for a lifetime of marital bliss shattered. I began to understand the normalcy I craved was never going to be a reality for me.

With the resulting divorce I became more introspective and confident. I made time to experience the freedom to explore my authentic self. Who was I, what was I, what was the purpose of my life? These were all feelings I had to explore, sometimes with much pain and sometimes with sheer joy. I remember shortly after breaking up walking through Macy's and watching elderly couples walking hand in hand. I just wanted to cry. I wanted *that* for me. In life some things are not to be; they're just different…that's the way it is.

CHAPTER EIGHTEEN

SURVIVING DIVORCE...

The divorce was a steppingstone to my first stage of authentic living and freedom. I had dated quite a bit and the women I dated were quality individuals. Again my mind continued to nag about the issue of attraction to men. It was a painful conflict between my ego and heart. I decided to go deeper and further explore the feelings and yearning. One of the reasons I didn't act on them in the past was that I felt the perpetrator who molested me would have won; that he helped make me 'that way'. I wasn't going to be like him! No way! I wasn't like him but the attraction to men became stronger.

It was an experience that had me trembling. I met a man at a gay bar and we were immediately attracted to each other. We went back to his home and I discovered what being romantic with a man was like. The guilt, shame, anger that I had about the molest still existed and exploded after this episode.

Seeking more psychological help I learned that acceptance of my feelings and who I am is critical to self-confidence. I needed to be honest with myself. I attended three years of group therapy with other men who were victims of molestation. There were men in this group who were beaten, abused and molested – a far worse scenario than mine.

The light bulb in my mind went off when the therapist used the word 'victimization.' I truly was a victim of that act, a victim forced into silence, and basically a victim of myself in the desire to be normal. The therapist was compelling in his desire for the men in the group to confront their perpetrators. In the beginning I wouldn't think of it. As time passed, I felt increasingly positive about accepting the therapist's suggestion and confront the man who changed my life. When it was done a tremendous sense of pride, relief, and the ability to feel I was in control my own destiny enveloped me. I also experienced a sense of forgivingness, a feeling I never anticipated. Emotional freedom was on its way.

Without a doubt I was beginning to know and accept the real me; the person who always felt different from everyone. The dissatisfaction with being different, of growing up in silence and being gay became *normal* for me. I finally learned and accepted that what is normal for one person is not for the other.

Individuality is blessed and we need recognize and honor our own uniqueness. The invisible strings of my self-imprisonment were being cut one at a time.

Prior to our divorce, I purchased a condo for Mom in a senior community in Orange County, CA. At first she was excited about moving away from NJ where she experienced much sadness. Although Myra was her daughter and lived nearby mother there was an absence of closeness between them. Myra would not allow mother to become dependant on her. Mother needed someone on whom she could depend and unquestionably it was I. Mother said she wanted 'a new life' and was content in living close to me. The concern for her well being was with me 24/7. As she grew older she became less social and was prone to complaining. Her complaining became so annoying that I could only visit her once a week for fear I'd lose my sanity. However, I called her daily via TDD to check in with her. I wanted Mom to make more friends and went to GLAD, Greater Los Angeles Deaf, a community organization dedicated to the deaf. It was there I was able to find and introduce her to some deaf people her age. Making friends was not easy for mom. In part, this was due to the fact that most of the deaf were proficient in sign language and she was not. I detected some difficulty in her ability to communicate. In addition, Mom was a rather judgmental soul and very much a perfectionist. Someone had better meet her standards or she would not invite them into her circle of friends. I remember that one of her criteria for making a person her friend was how clean their house was. No ifs, ands or buts, if the house wasn't immaculate she wouldn't allow the friendship to develop.

I always made a large effort to get Mom involved in social gatherings. Mom always complained she was lonely – and I felt guilty. I decided to invite my sister from NJ, along with her best friend and some of the deaf friends Mom had made in California to my home in Dana Point. We were eating brunch on the balcony and they were signing, laughing, and having a great time. Again I felt lost in the silence. But, this time was different. The difference was I no longer felt sorry for them, as I had as a child. I felt sorry for me for my lifetime of feeling sorry! I was the different one; the only hearing person in the group and not proficient in sign language. I wished I was encouraged to learn such a beautiful language; it would have made life much easier. I did, however, learn how to read lips. To this day I'm proud that I can read lips of a person quite some distance from me.

The tools the deaf have today would have made it much easier for my deaf family to be more independent. There are Blackberrys, TDDs, alarm clocks that vibrate, pagers, live video communication and more. Technology indeed has made its positive impact in the deaf world.

My thirst for success continued with the number one purpose to support my mother in grand style. Mom was rarely complimentary about my help. I believe she felt as though she were getting a handout.

After many years managing my business I began to lack the passion I previously had. There was little opportunity for my creative side to blossom. I stuck with it because I had Mom as a dependant.

It was the year 2000 and although my life was still at times tumultuous it was more stable than it had been in earlier years. In June of that year my beloved canine companion, Molley died at the age of four from cancer of the skull. Molley listened to me. She seemed to know what I was feeling. She knew my soul. With her passing I had a strong feeling my mother would be next. Mother was not ill; as a matter of fact she always struck me as strong as an ox. However, my intuition kept nagging me. It was Christmas Day, 2000 when we received her prognosis of terminal cancer. On February 2, 2001 Mom passed, eight months after Molley and my prediction.

The day she died was the day my life as I had always known it changed...forever. Her death didn't rock my boat; it capsized it. Who was I without Mother? Her ears were mine, her voice was mine, and her well-being was mine. She seemed permanently attached to me like a conjoined twin. The umbilical cord that made us one unit was severed. Could I breathe on my own? Could I truly be free? Could I finally be *me*? I was sad for Mother but she lived her life; she was eighty seven. I was sad for me, too. My whole self-image was predicated on being the ears and voice of the deaf.

Three months after Mom's passing Myra came to visit me. When talking with her I would cry when we talked about Mom. Myra's response was, "Ben, you are free, do you understand?" I had no idea how to extricate myself from the internal entanglement of caregiving. Even with Mom gone the feelings were still strong.

My self-image and who I am as a hearing man in a hearing world was about to be born. I was no longer a hearing man in a deaf world.

CHAPTER NINETEEN
A VICTIM OF MYSELF...

A friend of mine once said that we volunteer for circumstances that create our victimization. I feel that statement is partially correct. There are situations that we simply can't control; especially as children. As adults we can become victims of circumstances and victims of ourselves. We victimize ourselves when we fail to recognize we need to evaluate or own needs before taking care of another. Unconditionally giving our energy and ourselves to the care of another is a recipe for resentment, stress, and disaster if we're not careful. I was an example of this. I gave of myself totally and unconditionally without any thought to what it would do to me both emotionally and physically. It took a great toll on me.

As a caretaker my guilt and abnormal desire to fix and control everything for my family led to what I call serious 'addictive thinking.' There was a voice in my head continually reminding me of how my grandmother wanted me assume responsibility. I felt if I didn't adhere to her rules I wasn't a good person. At least the insidious voice inside me told me that!

My ego developed an addiction and attachment to the accolades I received by caring for my family. Relatives, friends and strangers would compliment me for being the one whom my family could depend. I had a sense of pride that generated my strong sense of self worth. I depended on that one area, caring for the deaf, to stroke my ego. "Aren't I wonderful!" the little voice in my head would say. "Wonderful" is based on who a person is without all the layers of ego that develop from childhood to maturity.

But, I was striving for achievement and recognition outside of being a caretaker. Although I reached most of my goals I wanted more and more and more. I never had the self-satisfaction and contentment I saw in many people. I didn't know who I was without responsibility and now without mother my dissatisfaction increased. With Mom's passing I should have experienced the freedom that Myra said I deserved. The freedom was slow to come; I was a victim of my own self perpetuating invisible ties that no longer existed.

It's still difficult for me to release the need for those ties. I seem to always want to help my family and friends when it would be preferable for them to help themselves. I have to consciously be aware of my need to control, 'fix', and resolve others problems.

When I first divorced, I realized I desperately needed and wanted freedom to discover the real me. So, I decided to reach for things I hadn't had the opportunity to because of my responsibilities. I went on vacation to Maui.

That was a mistake. It's a romantic island with couples outwardly displaying their affection for each other. Seeing this depressed me so that I considered jumping off the fourteenth floor balcony of my hotel

130

room. But, I fought through my feelings of 'aloneness' and became a better person (to myself) for it.

There was a strong and persistent need inside me to belong to the hearing world. I no longer had to straddle the worlds of deaf and hearing. I no longer was attached to a deaf person. I wanted the hearing world to be a part of me and me it. I wanted to shout 'here I am world look at me, HEAR *me*! The best vehicle for me to do this was my own voice, the voice that represented *my* spirit not anyone else's. The vehicle I chose was lecturing and singing.

During Christmas one year the men in my therapy group decided to try Karaoke. We found a quaint little tavern and all took turns at singing. When it was my turn there was no fear. It was a natural feeling for me. As I sang chills ran up and down my spine. I was able to express myself, to give of myself to the audience, and most of all to find joy. I learned that spiritually, giving and receiving are the same. This is what I felt when I sang. I gave my true self to the audience and the audience responded beautifully. I received attention for my talent and my spirit soaked it up. Singing helped me get in touch with my core being. I became a professional singer and to this day still get the chills up and down my spine as I did the first time I sang. I actually use the signs and expressiveness of the sign language that I know to act out what I'm singing. It is a unique way to emphasize the meaning of a song.

The audience is unaware of what I'm actually doing.

We become victims of ourselves when we aren't authentic. One must be true to himself and his emotions in order to achieve the freedom that authenticity provides. We live in a society that does, to this day, not easily accept people who are different. In order to resolve victimization we have to rise above the insecurity that can result from not "fitting in" to set cultural parameters. It's critical to create a self-assuredness based on the predication that our difference is the core of our individual authenticity. Although being different can be painful the bottom line is there is a specialness to it; something no one else has. No one has the same fingerprints, the same personality or uniqueness. It is in that uniqueness I have come to find joy.

I find it perplexing and sad that people poke fun of others because of their race, disability, looks, sexuality, and so on. If there is a God and he made us different from each other why would one feel the need to evaluate the difference of another? What self-serving purpose does it fulfill?

Victimization can be illusive. Sometimes we don't know we are victims until we are deep into bowels of it. One example of this is when I entered a new romantic relationship with a person I admired. He appeared to have everything I wanted in a partner. Two weeks after we met we were shopping in a store and he asked the cashier a question. He didn't like her response and screamed with a rage that was truly pathological. I thought of ending it right there but thought, oh well, he won't do that to me. WRONG.

The person I was thought I could help fix him. WRONG again. Slowly he started directing his anger and internal range towards me. I blindly stayed for almost two years after the realization that I truly was a victim in this relationship. After I ended it I realized, finally, that I am a survivor not a victim.

Victims say they 'can't. They can't leave, they can't take a vacation, and they can't put themselves first. Survivors say "I can." I found that when saying "I can't" I actually was saying "I won't." These phrases indicate the fear we feel and prevent progress. Survivors may have fear but they strive to push it aside and go for whatever their goal is. Victims perpetuate their victimization in an addictive way; *survivors end it.*

CHAPTER TWENTY

FROM VICTIM TO SURVIVOR

When I was young I didn't know I was a caregiver. I didn't know I had a 'title'. For me, assuming responsibility was normal. Didn't all children help their parents? I never gave it another thought. I didn't realize the extent of my care giving and the results that were to follow – I just followed instructions. I remember I was about four (when I started using the telephone) and people marveling at my ability to communicate with the deaf. I felt like a clown in the circus. I learned, being caregiver takes boundless compassion, energy, focus and almost infinite strength.

The stress of a caregiver can be both emotional and/or physical and takes on many forms. Feelings of frustration, anger, guilt, alienation, and exhaustion are the most common. Common symptoms are anxiety, irritability, social withdrawal, lack of concentration, and sleeplessness.

Stress is often described as the body's "fight or flight" response to danger. When the body goes on "high alert" to protect itself, essential functions, like respiration and heart rate, speed up, while less essential functions, such as the immune system, shut down. For caregivers, whose stress often results from fatigue and conflicts that never go away; their bodies never get a chance to heal. Stress affects the immune system and if it isn't functioning fully, the caregiver is at greater risk for infections and disease. Some experts believe that stress causes hypertension, coronary disease or even premature death. There was a time when the stress just about killed me. During my second episode with my illness caused by stress, my doctor said the results of my laboratory tests indicated I shouldn't be alive! He said I must be a very emotionally strong man. Was I? Oh, yes, indeed. I wanted to survive!

I've been asked if I would have preferred that my family be 'normal'. My family *was* normal until I learned otherwise by the definition of society and people who were not accepting of difference.

Many children of deaf adults (CODAs) have understanding friends or relatives who help them through the trials and tribulations of being a child of deaf adults. I did not. I had a dominant and caring grandmother who didn't understand the depth of emotional challenges I would grow into. She wanted insurance that the deaf people in her family were cared for. I was that insurance; this was the way it was supposed to be.

Although our family was, through need, functionally codependent I knew nothing different. The codependency was aggravated by the awareness at an early age that my parents' marriage was not a loving one. There wasn't a positive role model of relationships for me. I'm still discovering the basics of a loving relationship for myself.

As a victim and survivor I can say my life with the deaf has taught me the importance of not allowing others to become so dependant that they can't fare well without me. My ego doesn't need or want that anymore. I've learned no one actually has total control over anyone unless an individual wants that for some unhealthy reason. The deaf must be encouraged to be independent and successful members of society. I can remember when my parents met a deaf person who was a Peddler. A Peddler was one who would hand a person a card saying "DEAF – Please Help – Give Money" with a trinket attached to it. That was their job. My parents looked at these people in disgust and often lectured these Peddlers to **'GO TO WORK'** (although it was a difficult task for a person to find a good job in those days). Mother frowned in disgust and said firmly, **"not nice!"**

Do I miss the deaf community? I am a survivor of their silence. I survived the guilt, anger, ridicule, shame, and fear – all of it. The experience made me who I am today. Without a doubt, I've fulfilled the purpose of caring for my family over the period of fifty five years. That achievement, to me, is a magnificent contribution. When I'm feeling low I remind myself how I gave of myself for all that time. Yes, the experience was challenging yet the most giving act of love and devotion I could make to my family.

Because of my father, mother and sister, I am fearless of responsibility and compassion is my middle name. Most of all I discovered I could survive; I didn't have to or have the desire to remain a victim.

Nobody has to remain a victim. I had a passionate need to express myself, my emotions, and my voice. Today, I am my own voice and when I speak it is for me. Proudly, I became a well-known teacher - lecturer and my communication skills soar to the heavens as does my melodious voice. I found myself and my voice through the silence and survived.

AFTERLOGUE

I decided to write this book for a few reasons. It was truly a cathartic experience through which I shed many tears. I wanted share my story and make the point of how easy it is to become a victim of ourselves. My self actualization didn't start until I realized that I indeed was a self-made victim. As I indicated in the prologue, most CODAs [Children of Deaf Adults] become actively involved in the deaf community. I didn't take that route. I was 'burned out' being an advocate-care giver and it was critically important for me to discover my own authentic voice. To discover who I am I had to leave the past of my silent world for that of the hearing. I realized I would never be totally separate. There would always remain a special thread of connection between me and the deaf. I learned how tough the deaf can be. They were the strong ones.

The deaf are survivors, too. They meet the challenges of communication every waking moment. At times the attempt to achieve effective communication with the non-deaf can result in frustration. The frustration can result in confusion which culminates in over-emphasizing the issue at hand. It can be quite dramatic.

As a caretaker for fifty five years I earned my freedom from a life filled with a range of emotions both negative and positive.

I always felt my purpose in life was to care for and nurture others. I was born to fulfill some karmic requirement. My regrets and past hurts are mostly resolved now. I prefer to live in the present. I'm too old to hold grudges and regrets. Now is my time to care and nurture what *my* spirit craves, no matter how egocentric it appears. Caregivers have a hard and arduous road. If I were to give advice to caregivers, it is to exercise caution in handing over one's energy to another. Not knowing the real *you* other than being a caregiver can result in devastating repercussions.

When the need for caregiving ends it is a common desire to transfer those skills to another individual without consciously being aware of it. This is the case with my adult children. I had to separate myself for them. I had to consciously remember that I am not in control in their lives. I had to remember not to enable them because I was an enabler. Enabling behavior and controlling attachment is unhealthy. Although it is hard to separate, there needs to be at minimum emotional separation to remain objective and not lose oneself in the other's needs. Caregiving is a human act and a blessed one. But, who we are should never be defined by what we do for another at the expense of losing ourselves.

Last, but not least, I want to address the concept of difference. Difference is defined as a distinguishing characteristic, quality, feature, and so on. It takes on many forms in which one person differs from another. In our society we need greater compassion, understanding, and love toward

140

individuals who are different. Identifying and discovering the uniqueness and qualities of others is beautiful and exciting. No person should ever be considered 'less than' another if he/she is deaf, blind, impaired in any way, black, brown, yellow, gay, straight, or just plain different. Being different is no basis for being harassed, ridiculed or harmed. Different is just unique and offers us the opportunity to perceive others in many other dimensions. Difference is profound and beautiful in its own right.

Although my childhood had many tears I choose not to think of my childhood as totally sad. I served the purpose for which God placed me on earth. Metaphysicians often say we choose our parents [before we are born]. If I did, I'm glad I knew them. They depended on me, yes. Through helping them I learned to confront challenge in the face of many obstacles. They were beautiful people who did their best to live their lives. They depended on me and I learned about life and giving yourself to another. Giving is human, very human and Giving *is* Receiving.